REAL REVISION

AUTHORS' STRATEGIES TO SHARE WITH STUDENT WRITERS

KATE MESSNER

STENHOUSE PUBLISHERS
PORTLAND, MAINE

Stenhouse Publishers
www.stenhouse.com

Library of Congress Cataloging-in-Publication Data
Messner, Kate.
  Real revision : authors' strategies to share with student writers / Kate Messner.
     p. cm.
  Includes index.
  ISBN 978-1-57110-856-2 (pbk. : alk. paper) -- ISBN 978-1-57110-910-1 (e-book) 1.
English language--Composition and exercises--Study and teaching. 2. Motivation in
education. I. Title.
  LB1576.M457 2011
  808'.042071--dc22
                                                                    2010052894

Cover design, interior design, and typesetting by Blue Design (www.bluedes.com)

Manufactured in the United States of America

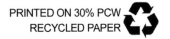

PRINTED ON 30% PCW
RECYCLED PAPER

17 16 15 14 13 12 11   9 8 7 6 5 4 3 2 1

For my mom, Gail Smith Schirmer, who has taught me so much about teaching, learning, and making art

CONTENTS

LIST OF MENTOR AUTHORS

Acknowledgments

This book came together in a whirlwind of goodwill, and I am most grateful to the following people for their help:

First and foremost, thanks to my seventh-grade students and families; my teaching colleagues at Stafford Middle School, especially my creative writing co-teacher Marjorie Light; and the administration of the Plattsburgh City School District for their support of this project.

To the creative people who gave me a glimpse inside their process: Sarah Albee, Tom Angleberger, Kathi Appelt, Nora Raleigh Baskin, Julie Berry, Elizabeth Bird, Loree Griffin Burns, Crissa Jean Chappell, Katie Davis, Karen Day, Erin Dionne, Kathryn Erskine, Deva Fagan, Jody Feldman, Greg Fishbone, Donna Gephart, Susan Goodman, Danette Haworth, Jennifer Holm, Matthew Holm, Sara Lewis Holmes, Rose Kent, Watt Key, Kirby Larson, Greg Leitich Smith, Cynthia Lord, Eric Luper, Nan Marino, Wendy Mass, Saundra Mitchell, Jim Murphy, Greg Neri, Mitali Perkins, Olugbemisola Rhuday-Perkovich, Lisa Schroeder, Suzanne Selfors, Joni Sensel, Rebecca Stead, Tanya Lee Stone, Linda Urban, Deborah Wiles, and Jane Yolen. Many thanks to you and your publishers for sharing the stories behind the work you do for kids. And thank you, always, for the gift of your writing.

My own publishers—Walker/Bloomsbury, Scholastic, and Chronicle—have also been incredibly supportive. Special thanks to editors Mary Kate Castellani and Anamika Bhatnagar for allowing me to share the stories behind the stories of the books we've made together. And thanks to literary agent Jennifer Laughran for her support, smarts, wit, and guidance in revision and beyond.

I'm grateful to editor Holly Holland for convincing me that I needed to write this book, and to Chris Downey, Chandra Lowe, Nancy Sheridan, and the entire smart, hardworking Stenhouse crew.

Finally, thanks to my family, Tom, Jake, and Ella—for everything, always.

Introduction

Dear teachers,

Dear teachers and writers,

Dear teachers who write and writers who teach,

Dear colleagues,

This is a book about revision. It's about real authors and how they revise the real books that are on your library shelves. It's full of secrets—revision tips and tricks that more than forty trade-book authors generously shared so that you can share them with your students.

Here's the first secret: Beverly Cleary and Judy Blume taught me how to write. There were other teachers, for sure. There was Don Edwards, the college journalism professor who showed me how to write TV news stories that matched the video. Before him, there was Mr. Smythe, the high school English teacher who noticed I was a pretty good writer but never let me get away with "pretty good" when I could do better. And before him, there was Mrs. Arnold, who tacked my grade school story about two kids in a snowstorm right up on the classroom bulletin board for everyone to see. I sat there during the math lesson staring at it, thinking that maybe I'd like to write more.

But before any of those other teachers, there were Beverly Cleary and Judy Blume. I'd never met them, but their dog-eared books lived on my nightstand. Their characters—Ellen Tebbits, Ramona, Peter, and Fudge—were as real to me as my classmates, and their words carried me through my childhood. These authors who were mentors from so far away taught me about dealing with mean kids, making mistakes, and making good. They taught me about writing descriptions so vivid you can smell the burning pancakes, about sentence structure, about stories and how they come together. For all of this, I am thankful.

The girl with the tattered copy of *Tales of a Fourth Grade Nothing* grew up to be a TV news reporter, and then a teacher and an author for kids. In 2006, I earned National Board Certification in Early Adolescent Language Arts, and my first nationally published children's book came out in 2009. These days, I'm writing books and teaching seventh-grade English at Stafford Middle School in upstate New York. Like many of you, I work at a school full of smart, dedicated teachers and staff members, fighting to help kids love reading, writing, and learning in a society that seems to be obsessed with test scores.

I hope this book will help.

Don't worry—I do talk about test writing, too. (It's on page 26 in case you need to show your administrator to get reimbursed for the book.) But mostly, this is a book to help kids write in the real world—the world that exists on the other side of the bubble sheets and number-two pencils, where writing isn't just about a first draft that follows the directions. Writing in that world—*my* world—is a process full of rethinking and scribbles and new ideas. It's about making meaning and sharing the human experience. For me, and for the author friends who share their revision stories here, it is also about joy. I have faith that if we teach kids this kind of writing, they'll do just fine on the test anyway.

I wore both of my hats—teacher and author—while I was writing this book. So you'll find stories from my writing room in the back of the house as well as stories from my classroom. You'll read about how I worked through the revision challenges of some of my own books. You'll find out that revising meant starting over from scratch with my Marty McGuire chapter-book series with Scholastic (2011). You'll read about returns to brainstorming and outlining, word-choice field trips, and what got left on the cutting-room floor when I revised middle-grades novels like *The Brilliant Fall of Gianna Z.* (2009), *Sugar and Ice* (2010), and *The Star Spangled Setup* (2012).

You'll also read about how I brought those manuscripts—my works-in-progress—into my seventh-grade classroom and other schools to talk with kids about the process of revision. I'll share the classroom activities I've developed as a result of my own revision strategies. And best of all, you'll hear from a whole crew of other children's writers who were kind enough to share their revision stories, too. Throughout this book, you'll find stories, strategies, and activities within each chapter and on special "author-mentor" pages with biographies and quotes provided by the authors, and on the "Try It" pages in the appendix. Share them with your students, and try them out with your own writing, too.

And let me know how it goes, okay? You can always drop me an e-mail through my Web site—www.katemessner.com. I'd love to hear how you're using these ideas in your classroom and in your own writing. In the meantime I'll be here, teaching and writing along with you.

All the best,

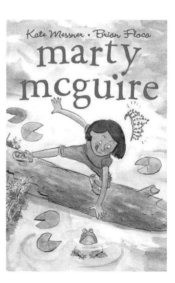

Revision Takes Wings

That old bird,
a croaker,
broad-backed,
broad-beaked,
is now a small
marbleized wren
singing like Elvis
from the top of the bush.
Does it matter
how he looks,
as long as he sings,
caroling us
to the next sentence,
leading us on
paragraph to paragraph,
to the final full-throated
stop.
Revision is like that,
seeing the bird
anew,
remodeling,
remarking,
remaking him
till he sings
and wings himself
right
off
the printed page.

—JANE YOLEN (2006)

CHAPTER 1

Real Revision: Where Stories Start to Sing

I t's the third morning of a heat wave in northern New York State. My husband has taken our daughter to her skating lesson, and the house is quiet. This is prime work time, but my thoughts are everywhere except on the novel I am supposed to be revising.

I open the file, putter for a little while, and check my e-mail. No new messages.

I get another cup of coffee.

I look at the manuscript again. This is hard. And it's too hot. We are not supposed to have heat waves here in almost-Canada.

I should probably go back and look at those revision notes I made yesterday.

Watermelon would be good right now.

I am doing everything *but* working. I am the same teacher who will urge, encourage, coax, prod, and cajole my seventh graders to revise. "It's not so hard," I'll tell them. And they'll look at me with those skeptical, don't-know-you-quite-yet September eyes. Because they already know the truth: Revising *is* hard.

Getting to the end of a writing project can seem overwhelming, like one of those restaurant bowls of pasta that you keep eating and eating but never empty. I revise and revise, and yet the tasks keep spilling over the edges of my brain. And I have many, many published author friends who feel the same way.

But we have some secret weapons, some tips and tricks of the trade that break that overwhelming mess into a series of manageable jobs. We accomplish these jobs and we feel capable again, like good writers who can revise even in ninety-five-degree heat. Even when there's no more watermelon.

We can adapt many of those same strategies for use in our classrooms, to help students feel more confident and competent about writing and revising.

• • •

Just what is revision, anyway? Sometimes I think it's best to define revision by talking about what it isn't, so let me take you back to a conversation I had with a middle school student who was finishing a piece of writing.

"I need to add a few more mistakes," he said. "Then I can print."

Say *what*?

"You're *adding* mistakes?"

He nodded, pecking away at the keyboard.

When I asked him why, he explained that the teacher was giving a score based on how well students revised the draft. "She said we won't get a good grade unless she sees that we've corrected spelling mistakes on this draft, but I was editing as I went along, so I had to go back and add stuff to fix." He clicked the print button. "There. Now I can revise the way she wants us to."

I bit my tongue because as much as I'd like to say that I can't understand how a teacher could encourage this kind of "revision," I understand all too well how it happens. With the increased emphasis on high stakes testing in the area of English/language arts, we often have little time for the reflection that real revision requires. Revision is, by its very definition, the act of seeing something again. And in order to see something again, you need to stop looking at it for a little while, at least, and have time to think anew.

My debut novel for young readers, *The Brilliant Fall of Gianna Z.*, was released from Walker/Bloomsbury in September 2009. When our UPS guy delivered the first author copies to my door, I opened the box and stared. The book had brilliant, bright artwork on the dust jacket and my name under the title. But I thought it should have had something else, perhaps a tiny label to let kids know they were reading a story that had taken three years to grow from an idea to a title on library shelves.

I wonder if most young readers believe that their favorite authors sit down each day and pour out perfectly crafted books in between sips of tea. It doesn't work that way. Not for me and not for any writer I've ever met.

Revision involves rethinking not what a piece of writing is, but what it might become. It requires time to consider roads not traveled in the first draft. It often involves collaboration and discussion. It can include sticky notes, index cards, computerized comments, colored pencils, highlighters, and messes. Always messes. And always time. As teachers, if we wish to teach real-world writing, we need to find a way to make room for all of that.

Real revision won't happen with every piece of writing on every day, but perhaps students could choose one piece of writing every quarter to put through the full process—the kind of process that has room for reflection and real reimagining. Perhaps we could work toward a classroom where every piece of writing goes through some measure of real revision so that students have that transformative experience of stepping back from the page, seeing it in a new way, then getting back to work.

With time and tools, support from mentors and friends, revision can actually be fun. In the coming chapters, we'll talk about how to make it happen. You'll find many revision stories from authors who write the books that your students read. You'll find stories about characters who were deleted and whole chapters that got cut. You'll find stories about choosing the right words and getting rid of the wrong ones, about making some scenes longer and others shorter, about bringing people and places to life. And you'll find stories about the hard parts, the dark, scary revision places and the strategies that served as ladders leading into the light again.

I hope you'll also find inspiration. Revision is where writing really happens. It's often the most challenging, hair-pulling, watermelon-wishing part of the writing process. I also think it's the most rewarding.

Revision is where stories start to sing. Where lumpy writing gets smoothed out and where good writing turns into great writing. It's the part where the real magic happens.

Revision is like drawing because you erase and shade in the details.

—CHRISSA CHAPPELL*

CHAPTER 2

Creating a Revision-Friendly Classroom

During a four-day summer writing retreat on the shores of Lake Champlain, twenty-two authors who write for kids and teens gather to work, share stories, and talk about the challenges that only other writers understand. We also eat a fair amount of dessert, fuel for the long hours of writing.

After breakfast, many of us take half an hour for exercise. Some have shorter attention spans than others, and sitting all day is hard. One day, a yoga instructor comes, and we clear the chairs from the big living room, unroll mats and towels, and stretch. That's the idea here, after all, to stretch in new directions.

"Hold one arm out straight from your body," the instructor says, "and push back on your fingers. Stretch that wrist. Do this when you finish at your keyboards today, too."

In our final relaxation pose, she reminds us to take deep breaths. "And think about what you'll write later on."

Quiet writing time settles on the inn like fog. In every room, chairs are filled with barefoot writers, feet tucked underneath them, computers in their laps, fingers tapping keyboards or frozen in midair while someone stares at the knotted wood in the ceiling beams, looking for answers. (See Figure 2.1.)

*Unless otherwise noted, all quotes are based on personal or online interviews with the author.

FIGURE 2.1
Writers settle into quiet revision time.

I'm working in the quiet room now, the enclosed porch with the ceiling fans that we designated as a spot for people who want to work in complete silence. If you're here, you're not available to chat or take a break for ladder golf on the lawn right now; you're working, and that's respected.

There are six of us this afternoon, spaced out around tables arranged in a horseshoe pattern. Cindy is drafting a new middle-grades novel, poking at her keyboard with one hand, the other cupping her chin in concentration. Alyson is a new writer, joining us for the first time this year. She's been journaling most of the week and is just now starting to turn scribbles into story. Julie sits across from me, her red curls corralled in a bandana to keep them out of her face. She leans over her laptop screen and looks like she's trying not to laugh out loud. She's drafting her fourth Splurch Academy book this morning—a funny chapter-book series, so it's no wonder she's smiling while she thinks. Jeramy is frowning at his computer; maybe it's a darker scene he's writing or just one that's giving him particular trouble. I'll ask him later at lunch, when we will all talk again. And next to me, Erin is pounding out her fifth revision of a novel about marching band. She has iPod buds in her ears and is listening to a sound track she picked especially for this project. She pauses every so often to look at the notebook beside her—a mix of character notes, time lines, and reminders from Erin to Erin that this revision, tough as it may be, is within reach.

Throughout the retreat we've had breaks to check e-mail, walks to skip stones by the lake, and a particularly rousing beach volleyball game one night, but mostly, we've shared quiet writing time and loud celebrations of our progress at mealtime. One thing that strikes me is how many of us might be struggling if there were more rules at this place. What if you couldn't have any music while you revised? Would Erin be working so long, so well? What if you could take breaks only at certain times—instead of when you were at a good stopping place and needed one? What if we didn't have a quiet room?

Yesterday, Joan and I sat on a flat rock in the sun—it wasn't long, maybe half an hour—and talked about ideas for new books. "And what if . . . And what if . . . And what if then . . . ?" It was the kind of conversation you have in kindergarten, making up the game of pretend house or school.

Is it fair to expect great writing in settings that don't allow some flexibility? Some time for quiet, some time for talk, and some time for play? And how might we work some of this into our classrooms?

As a teacher, the most successful writing days with my students have not been the days I spent in front of a quiet classroom. Our happiest, most productive times have occurred during our writing workshops, when kids are doing the real work of writers—drafting, researching, brainstorming, revising, mapping, charting, doodling, talking (yes, talking!), thinking, reading, starting over, researching again, and playing. Such periods might have looked a little chaotic when the principal walked by, and they certainly weren't times when everyone was doing the same thing or following the same schedule. While the looser environment can make many of us feel uncomfortable because we seem to have less control in the classroom, I have experienced the rewards, both as an author and as a writing teacher. Looking around this old inn on Lake Champlain, relishing the setting and the richness of our time together, I feel more committed than ever to offering students the same gift of time to write, to think, to revise.

In the Classroom

We can't take our students on writing field trips to rambling inns, so how can we best recreate this kind of setting within the walls of school? Here are some thoughts:

FLEXIBILITY

Recognize that the revision process might look different for different students and even for the same student from project to project. Revision might involve going back to the outline, creating character charts, freewriting, or mapmaking. It might involve scissors and index cards, or sticky notes and colored pencils. The more flexibility we can give kids in terms of how they revise, the more we make the process seem like it might work for every learner.

SPACE

Sometimes, when I'm revising, I take up the entire kitchen table and half the counter. Revising means taking time to look at what you've already done—all of it—so it helps if you can set aside space in your classroom for spreading out. Options can include pushing a big table against a wall or designating a spot on the carpet where students know they can organize or rearrange some papers and think.

QUIET PLACES AND TALKING PLACES

During revision time, it may also help to designate areas of the classroom for silent work and other places where it's okay to have a quiet writing conference. That way, students can move between the two places, depending on where they are in the writing process and what their needs are.

PLACES TO MOVE

As a teacher who often has trouble sitting still, I have a special place in my heart for the wigglers and the chair tippers in my classroom. Yes, we need to have rules to keep kids safe, and the chair tipping probably needs to be replaced with something else, but I really believe some students need to move around in order to think and write effectively. Is it all right with you if students stand while they work or kneel on a chair? Is there a place in your classroom where a student could pace back and forth a little while he or she thinks through a writing problem?

MATERIALS

In one corner of my seventh-grade classroom, I keep a writing center stocked with supplies that anyone can borrow or use as needed. Here's a list of some materials that may be helpful in a classroom where real revision happens:

- Paper (lined and unlined)
- Larger paper for maps/outlines/graphic organizers
- Pencils
- Colored pencils
- Highlighters
- Sticky notes
- Scissors
- Clear tape
- Index cards
- Rulers

Once you have the colored pencils and index cards, you'll need something else to make your classroom truly revision friendly. Unfortunately, the next item on the list is more difficult to come by than sticky notes. It's something they don't sell at office supply stores: time.

TIME

Making time during the school day, at least some time, is essential to persuade students that revision matters. If it's important enough for you to devote twenty minutes a day, or half an hour a week, or whatever regular time you can provide, you convey the expectation that revision will happen. We'll talk more about how to find that time in Chapter 3.

Kirby Larson

Kirby Larson went from historyphobe to history fanatic thanks to hearing a snippet of a story about her great-grandmother homesteading in eastern Montana. That bit of family lore inspired her to write *Hattie Big Sky* (2006), a young-adult historical novel, which is a 2007 Newbery Honor Book. In 2006, she began collaborating with her dear friend Mary Nethery, a partnership that has so far produced two nonfiction picture books. The first, *Two Bobbies: A True Story of Hurricane Katrina, Friendship, and Survival* (2008), illustrated by Jean Cassels, won both the 2008 ASPCA Henry Bergh Award and the 2009 SIBA Award and has received six state reading awards. Their second joint project (with Major Brian Dennis), *Nubs: The True Story of a Mutt, a Marine & a Miracle* (2009), spent more than two months on the *New York Times* best-seller list, is a Christopher Award winner, and has been nominated for half a dozen state reading awards. Kirby has also written two new historical novels. *The Fences Between Us* (2010) is set during World War II, and *The Friendship Doll* (2011) takes place over a ten-year period during the Great Depression. She lives in Kenmore, Washington, with her patient husband and Winston the Wonder Dog. Her Web site is http://www.kirbylarson.com.

I bought a rock tumbler a few months back and have realized rock tumbling and writing have a lot in common. There are four to six steps involved in polishing a stone, and each step can take a week or more, using finer and finer grit. Near the end of each step, I pull out one rock to evaluate the process of the entire batch. Does it still have rough edges? Back into the tumbler it goes. Just when I think I'm finally finished—after those many steps—I pull out yet another stone and rub it gently on a bit of cerium oxide. If I see a shine, the batch is done. Otherwise, I need to keep polishing. I see writing like this. Each step requires a different tool. In the early stages, the tools are rougher—maybe going back to my research notes for a telling detail or trying a scene in another point of view to make sure I'm telling the story from the proper perspective. As I near the end of the polishing process, the tools get finer—maybe I'll make a list of words about airplanes/flying to reflect the passion of one of my characters and look for ways to incorporate those words into the text; maybe I'll see if I can cut ten words from a page.

TRY IT

If revising is like rock tumbling, what do the early and later stages look like? Try this progressive to-do list with your own writing.

Early Tumbling/First Steps

- What did I want this piece of writing to be about? Does it do that job?
- Are there big sections/paragraphs/scenes that don't seem to fit? Cut them.
- Where could I add more detail and description?
- Does the voice of this piece feel real when I read it aloud?

Keep Tumbling/Middle Steps

- Do the characters in my writing feel like real people? How can I make them more interesting?
- Are there factual details that I need to check? Do I need to do a little more research?
- When I think about organization, does this piece make sense? Do the details of the time line work? Could I put the events on a time line or calendar to check?
- Where might I add more detail (again!)?
- Have I included language that appeals to all five senses?

Polishing/Fine Tuning

- Are there extra words that I can cut?
- Are my verbs active and precise?
- Are my nouns specific and concrete?
- Can I get rid of adverbs and replace them with stronger verbs?
- If I read my piece out loud, are there sentences that make me stumble? How can I make those sentences flow more smoothly?
- Finally (when all the other polishing is done), have I proofread my story to make sure I've used correct grammar, spelling, punctuation, and capitalization?

Revision is like a second
chance because it lets you
discover what you were
trying to say all along.

—SUSAN GOODMAN

CHAPTER 3

The Elephant in the Room (And It's Ticking Away the Minutes!)

Certainly, if you've picked up this book, you think good writing is important. You want to help students revise and make their writing as strong as possible. But your classroom is busy. You have a lot going on.

If you teach at the secondary level, you already have more days in the curriculum than you do on the actual calendar, and you see those students for only forty minutes or eighty minutes a day, and then sometimes they leave for music lessons to boot. I know; I've had fantasies about keeping my seventh graders all day, locking the doors and making faces at the math and science teachers through the window while I finish what I wanted to do in English.

If you teach at the elementary level, lunch count, attendance, and possibly boots and snowsuits in the winter already eat up a chunk of your morning. Physical education; enrichment classes; and state standards to meet in math, science, and social studies, in addition to language arts, claim more instructional time. And let's not even talk about the days you already have to give up for testing and teacher meetings. How are you supposed to complete a rigorous writing assignment, much less ask your students to work on second and third drafts?

Finding time for an authentic revision process within the regular school day is a challenge, but I'd argue that it's worth the effort. Try to take at least one piece of writing through a complete revision process each quarter of the school year. Other pieces can go through shorter revision processes—ten- or fifteen-minute workshops that focus on improving word choice, organization, or voice.

Ask any award-winning author what an early draft looks like. You'll hear words such as *crummy, lousy, rough, a mess* (and those are the mildest of the bunch!). It's during the revision process that the real work of writing—the work of *good* writing—happens. If we're not making time for that part of the process, are we really teaching writing?

In a perfect world, this is where I'd wave the magic wand that adds two hours to your school day so you can get everything done. Or maybe there would be a secret entrance to an enchanted revision chamber where school-day time stands still. You could go there with your students and have all the time in the world for deep revision, stepping back into the real world only when the drafts were polished and sparkling. But because this is a teacher resource book and not a teacher fantasy, the best I can do is offer some ideas on how to make the most of the time you already have.

However you carve out time for revision, try to give students a little space between their drafts and the revision process. The very makeup of the word *revision*—re-vision—suggests the process of first looking away so that it's possible to see writing in a new light. And looking away takes time. Many authors say they need to put a manuscript away for a period of time before they're ready to begin the revision process; it helps them see their own writing with fresh eyes.

Poet Kelly Fineman, whose work has been published in *Highlights for Kids*, calls it giving a poem time to rest and says, "It could be as little as half an hour or as long as a year, but I need to have established some sort of distance from it in order to read it at least somewhat objectively and not like a doting author."

Watt Key, the author of *Alabama Moon* (2006) and *Dirt Road Home* (2010), generally needs to walk away from his novels for several weeks before returning to revise. "I will work on unrelated short stories during this time. During this break, I will typically begin to realize ways to fix parts of my novel that have been bothering me," he says. "I let these realizations build until I am ready to get back to work."

Jim Murphy says taking a break from his nonfiction manuscripts is like going on vacation and then returning. "When you get back home, it seems a little strange and foreign, and you notice things . . . the chair in the corner is too far from the wall. Why didn't you see that before? Because you were so familiar with the chair-wall relationship that it seemed right. The same thing happens when I take a vacation from a text. When I get back to reading it, it seems as if someone else wrote the words, and I can see every mistake, repetition, incomplete thought, and odd word choice."

How might we give students a vacation from their writing in the classroom? Is there any reason why we can't assign a piece of writing and then put it away for a week or two after the drafts are complete? Students could go on and work on their other studies, and after the manuscripts have had that rest period, they could take them out again, take part in a few mini-lessons on the revision process, and get back to work with new eyes.

From Start to Finish

Let's take a look at the revision time line for my first novel for young readers, *The Brilliant Fall of Gianna Z*, published in 2009 (see Figure 3.1).

A Revision Time Line for *The Brilliant Fall of Gianna Z.*

September 2006: I start work on a book called *Swinger of Birches*, about a girl and a leaf collection.

April 2007: I finish my draft, revise it, and send the revised draft to my critique group.

April–July 2007: I revise again. I start sending the book to agents to see if one might want to represent me and help me find an editor.

July 2007–August 2007: A handful of agents say, "No thanks." Some offer ideas to make the story better. I revise again.

August 2007: Another agent says "No thanks"; the story starts too slowly and takes too long to get to the good parts. I send her a thank-you note. Then I cut the first three chapters out of the book. I highlight the sections of those chapters that were truly important and find other places to include those bits of text. Chapter 4 is now the new Chapter 1.

September 2007: I send the new manuscript to several more agents, including one new agent who sounds amazing. Just by reading her blog, I can tell she's as passionate and knowledgeable about books as anyone I've ever known. I cross my fingers.

November 2007: That new agent calls to tell me she likes my book and would love to represent me. She'd like me to come up with a new title though. . . .

December 2007: I sign a contract with agent Jennifer Laughran with Andrea Brown Literary. I start brainstorming new titles. Jennifer sends an e-mail asking if I'm attached to the bits of poetry I've chosen to begin each chapter. She thinks the book might be stronger if we just got rid of them. I send a note back. I am very attached to those passages. They stay, for now. We decide on a new title—*Maple Girl*—and Jennifer begins sending the book out to editors.

FIGURE 3.1

December 2007–February 2008: Two editors say "No thanks." One offers to take another look at the manuscript if I revise again. She suggests adding more school scenes and bringing Zig into the story more. I make notes on this and wait to see if there's more feedback before beginning a new revision.

February 2008–May 2008: A few more editors say "No thanks," and some make suggestions for revision. I write a new draft of *Maple Girl*, and Jennifer sends it out to other editors.

June 2008: Editor Mary Kate Castellani at Walker Books for Young Readers makes an offer on the book to publish it in fall 2009. We accept, and Mary Kate sends an extensive revision letter (see Figure 3.2), detailing changes she'd like me to consider within the manuscript. She wants me to start brainstorming a new title.

FIGURE 3.2

Editor Mary Kate's first revision letter

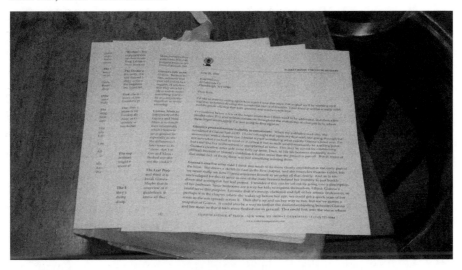

July 2008: I work on another round of revisions that involve exploring the relationship between Gianna and her mother, increasing the tension in one of the scenes with Gianna's Nonna, describing Gianna's bedroom so readers can see her character more clearly, adding scenes with secondary characters Ellen and Ruby, and cutting several scenes that go on too long. Also, Mary Kate asks, could we consider getting rid of those bits of poetry at the beginning of the chapters? They don't fit all that well. . . . I write Jennifer an e-mail, tell her she was right about the darn quotes, and delete them.

I also ask everyone I know to help me brainstorm new titles: *Catch a Falling Leaf*; *The Leaf Game*; *How to Catch a Falling Leaf*; *Cookie Crumbs in the Coffins*; *25 Leaves by Friday*; and *Paparazzi, Picasso, and 25 Dumb Leaves* are all considered and rejected. Agent Jennifer offers up one last possibility: *Gianna and the Terrible, Horrible, No Good, Very Bad Title*. She is only half kidding.

August 2008—September 2008: A new title is chosen: *The Brilliant Fall of Gianna Z.* Editor Mary Kate sends another letter with more line edits, and I work on another round of revisions that involve increasing the tension in certain scenes and making sure Gianna's emotional response matches what's happening. Mary Kate also asks for more New England/autumn flavor in the book and asks me to take another look at the relationship between Gianna and Zig to make sure it's evolving in a way that feels natural.

November 2008: The copyeditor has reviewed the manuscript and made notes on almost every page. I spend a few weeks reading through, answering questions, and approving changes. Who knew that *shoe box* had to be two words? I send my notes back to New York.

December 2008: The manuscript comes back to me again with more editing notes. I review, make comments, and send it back.

January 2009: The production editor has read through the copyedited manuscript and has a few more questions. For example, in one spot, I wrote that Gianna's grandmother separated "three strands of hair for a French braid." Shouldn't that be three sections? You can't make a braid with just three strands, right? We change it.

February 2009: Page proofs arrive in a big envelope. The proofs look like a photocopied version of the book's pages, and corrections can still be made at this stage. I proofread and find twenty-two changes that need to be made, including a couple of typos, missing quotes, an inconsistency in where Gianna says she left her backpack, a comma error, and a few other changes that weren't necessary but that improved the text.

April 2009: Advance Reader Copies (ARCs) are printed, and we discover two more corrections that need to be made—one typo and one inconsistency. They're fixed.

June 2009: Final pass page-proof notes are sent back and forth with more corrections being made. And with that, the process ends. Final pages are sent for printing to be ready for the September 1 release date!

September 1, 2009: The Brilliant Fall of Gianna Z. is published—three years after I started writing it.

As you can see, the novel revision process can go on for many, many months and take on many different forms. My revision process for this novel included traditional activities such as replacing tired words with more vivid ones and checking for consistency within the story. But it also included throwbacks to what most people think of as earlier phases of the writing process—brainstorming, research, and outlining. All of those elements can be part of student revisions, too, just on a smaller scale.

Colonial America Diary: A Classroom Example

In my seventh-grade English classroom, we make time for revision during our regular class periods whenever the students are working on a major writing project. Classes are eighty-four minutes long, and I see my students every other day. One of our whole-class writing/research projects is the Colonial America Diary that ties in with our American History social studies standards. This research-based, historical fiction assignment asks students to create their own character who might have been alive in the years leading up to the American Revolution. A student might choose to take on the role of a thirty-four-year-old farmer's wife in Connecticut, a fifty-eight-year-old Quaker minister in Pennsylvania, a fourteen-year-old printer's apprentice in New York, or any number of other colonial identities. The students research every aspect of their character's life, using library, Internet, and other sources, and they write a series of five diary entries from days in that character's life, incorporating the research. We display the projects at a Colonial Tavern Celebration for families, where students may also choose to create models, perform colonial-era music, dress up as their characters, and serve colonial-era foods.

I work collaboratively with the social studies teacher on my team for this unit. Before students begin the writing project, we explore the history of the English colonies and read at least one historical novel set in the same time period. (Laurie Halse Anderson's *Chains* [2008] and *Fever: 1793* [2000] are among our favorites.) This enables students to see strong models of historical writing that incorporates research into a character's personal story. Throughout the unit, we continue to read examples of historical fiction during our shared read-aloud time, and early on, we let students know that they'll be choosing their own characters to write about. We want them to match their interests to their writing topics so they will have a good idea of what they'd like to do when it's time to start writing.

Here's a sample of what our writing-project time line might look like for the colonial diaries:

DAY 1: PROJECT INTRODUCTION

Students receive project packets that include the following:

- A step-by-step guide to completing the writing assignment
- A research worksheet with questions to investigate and space for students to generate their own
- A page for writing down source information for use in a bibliography
- An outline template with space for students to fill in a topic and related notes for each day of their diary
- A writer's revision checklist
- A partner revision checklist
- A sample diary entry that models strong writing in this genre
- A rubric outlining expectations for four focus areas
  - Ideas and research
  - Organization
  - Voice and word choice
  - Conventions and presentation

After we go over the project packet and have mini-lessons on starting research and note taking, students select their colonial characters and brainstorm questions, key words for searching, and possible sources for their research.

DAYS 2-4: GUIDED RESEARCH

These days are a mix of library-based mini-lessons and student research time. I collaborate with our school librarian, watching for student needs and designing on-the-fly mini-lessons on everything from a review of using an index to advanced searching of historical newspaper databases, depending on the student needs we observe.

DAY 5: CONTINUED RESEARCH AND PLANNING

By now, students are starting to feel like they have what they need to begin writing, so we invite them to do some planning for what they'll talk about on each day of their character's diary. This allows students to take stock of what they have and go back to gather more information on anything they might be missing.

DAYS 6-8: DRAFTING

I begin our drafting days with a demonstration, starting with a page of notes projected on our classroom interactive whiteboard. I use these notes to write a sample diary entry, thinking aloud as I write so that students can see the process a writer might go through in deciding what information to include and how to make it seem like a seamless part of the story rather than a random fact.

I'm fortunate to teach in a school that has a computer lab that can be signed out for classroom use, so for these drafting days, I plan ahead, sign out a big block of time, and have my students write their first drafts right on the computer. I find this saves time, facilitates the revision process, and eliminates the "I'll copy it over more neatly" mind-set when it comes to revision. If that's not possible and students need to draft by hand, I recommend having them skip lines and leave wide margins on each side for the kind of thoughts-in-the-spaces that are part of a meaningful revision process.

While my students draft, I ask them to turn off the word-processing feature that immediately highlights misspelled or grammatically incorrect words. Too many of them find it impossible to finish a sentence with that squiggly red line staring them in the face, and stopping every few lines to run spell-check really gets in the way of fluent writing.

If they run into problems while they're drafting (and who doesn't?), I encourage them to keep an ongoing revision list—a scribbled page of things they know they want to go back to once we start revising. Often during this project, students will be writing along and suddenly realize they need more information, and I invite them to write notes to themselves within the manuscript as revision reminders, too. For example, one of my students was writing a scene in which her colonial character's child was sick with yellow fever, but she had no idea yet what the symptoms of this disease would have been. I showed her a strategy I often use in my own writing: leaving notes to yourself in a different color—or all caps or boldface—to facilitate revision later on.

> It has been a long winter, and I fear my daughter has fallen ill. She is (WHAT ARE THE
> SYMPTOMS OF YELLOW FEVER????) and I worry that the other children may be next.

A quick note like this serves two purposes. It enables the writer to stay in the flow of drafting and also provides a great starting place for the revision process after that draft is complete.

DAY 9: BACK TO THE LIBRARY

By now, some students will be finished drafting. Others may still have more work to do, and some of them will be using time during study halls or after school to finish while we begin to revise. I schedule a back-to-the-library day because almost all students discover while writing that they need more information. They need to know what those yellow fever symptoms are or, if the person in the diary dies of yellow fever, what funeral practices were like in the eighteenth century. Our back-to-the-library day also focuses on gathering more specific details, which students may use to enrich scenes during the revision process.

Depending on our schedule, we might take a break from the project entirely at this point for a couple of days to work on other independent writing or reading, literature circles, or a shared reading. That affords students the opportunity to have a little time away from their writing so that when they return to revise, they have more objectivity.

DAYS 10-11: REVISING ON YOUR OWN

Students take this day to incorporate their back-to-the-library notes and begin to work on the tasks on their writer's revision checklists (see Figure 3.3). I model these activities on the whiteboard at the beginning of class.

Revision Checklist

Keep this handout in your binder for a general revision checklist!

When you finish typing a draft:

- Read your introduction out loud. Does it grab attention?
- If your introduction says "I am going to tell you..." "My essay..." "In this piece of writing..." "You will learn..." or anything like that, change it to something more compelling.
- Read your conclusion out loud. Does it provide a satisfying ending?
- If your conclusion says "I have now told you..." "My essay..." "In this essay..." "Now you know..." or anything like that, change it to a stronger ending.
- Read your entire paper out loud. Mark places where you stumbled or had a tough time reading aloud. These are places where you'll want to look at your sentence fluency.
- Check to see if your sentences are different lengths. Some should be longer, while others are short and crisp. You may want to break up some sentences or combine others to improve sentence fluency.
- Find words in your essay that are dull (walked, nice, good, fun, etc.) Replace them with more vivid, precise words. Try to find at least a few spots in each paragraph where you can make your language more vivid and precise.
- When you read your paper out loud, did it sound like you? Are there places where you could adjust the language you use or add some ideas to make sure your personality shows through in your writing?

FIGURE 3.3
A general revision checklist

DAY 12: PARTNER REVISION

By now, most students are feeling "all revised out" and don't have much energy left for this part of the process. I know how they feel. After spending months writing and revising a novel, I always reach a point where I feel as if I've done everything that I can possibly do and I'm just changing the word *the* to *a* and back again. At that point, I know it's time for the manuscript to go to my critique group or editor, time for fresh eyes to read it and see what I might have missed. When I get the manuscript back with comments, I always get a second wind, a new burst of energy for the book I thought I had finished, and it ends up better than I could have made it alone.

Having students work collaboratively during the revision process can bring about this same kind of second wind, so this day is dedicated to partner revision. I ask students to use a partner revision checklist as they read someone else's diaries (see Figure 3.4).

Global Citizens Colonial Tavern Diaries
Revision Checklist

Does the diary include:

- A detailed description of the person's work?
- A detailed description of the person's home life?
- A detailed description of the colony in 1750, including important events or people?
- At least 5 entries with 100 words each?
- At least two paragraphs in each of the 5 diary entries?

If this writer is missing any of these required elements, please explain below:

- Where does this writer need to add more historical detail? (mark a D on the paper)

- Where has this writer written something that you don't quite understand? (mark a ? on the paper)

- Where might this writer need to start a new paragraph? (mark a P on the paper)

FIGURE 3.4

A partner revision checklist for the Colonial America Diary project

Students leave comments, either in the margins on a paper copy of the diary or using the comments feature of Microsoft Word (see Chapter 16) if we're working on computer screens. This takes most of the double period, but we reserve the last few minutes for students to go back to their own computers, read comments, and ask questions to clarify any comments that need further elaboration. This sets us up for our final day of revision.

DAY 13: REVISING ON YOUR OWN (AGAIN!)

Students make use of the partner comments to make another round of revisions. They also complete a self-evaluation, based on the rubrics in their project packets, to see where their writing might still be improved.

DAY 14: EDITING DAY

Today is dedicated to cleaning up the details. Students complete the editing tasks at the bottom of their revision checklists to run through a series of activities designed to tidy the spelling, grammar, punctuation, and usage. Using a computer spell-check is part of this process, although not the first step, and I always give a mini-lesson on how to use spell-check effectively. Chapter 14 discusses the final editing process in more detail.

DAY 15: PUBLICATION DAY

We address last-minute details and print our diaries today. By now, it's the eve of our Colonial Tavern Celebration, so students are also planning for their final presentations.

This time line represents six weeks of my teaching life. A long stretch to devote to one project? You bet. Worth the time? I sure think so. In our end-of-the-year reflections, my students inevitably comment on the Colonial America Diary project as one of their favorites of the year, the most challenging they've ever done, and often their strongest piece of writing.

That said, we don't take this kind of time to revise every single piece of writing. In fact, most of my students' writing projects are smaller in scale, and we generally focus on one writing trait through a shorter revision process. Our persuasive essays involve just two days of revision—one for working on elaboration and supporting ideas with facts, and one for strengthening leads and conclusions. Our poetry revision activities focus on the use of vivid language and include several revision activities that can be completed in just ten or fifteen minutes.

If you can manage to do a really thorough revision process for even one piece of writing each school year and do some revision with each final draft piece of writing, you're on the road to being a revision superstar. While some of the activities in this book are best suited for a full class or lesson period, most will work within shorter periods of time, and many can be adapted to fit into those few minutes before lunch.

Timed Tests and Revision

Inevitably, in the midst of one of my favorite revision activities, one surly seventh grader will look up from the index cards and colored pencils and ask the question, "Why are we doing all this when we won't have time for any of it on the state test?"

My answer is always some version of this: "I'm not getting you ready for the test. I'm getting you ready for the world. The test is just something that happens along the way."

The surly, test-mentioning students are right in one sense. There's generally little time to revise the kinds of writing on standardized tests. For this reason, I tend to teach "test writing" as a separate genre. It carries a different set of rules and, quite frankly, a different purpose, which is earning points. So when I teach test writing, I teach single-draft writing, usually preceded by a quick planning session aimed at the goal of earning points on a rubric. This is an effective strategy that doesn't get in the way of teaching the more meaningful writing skills that are useful in the wide world beyond standardized tests.

If students have ten or fifteen minutes left at the end of a timed test-writing session, they can apply a few quick revision techniques to make a test response stronger.

- *Bonus Detail.* Reread each paragraph, and try to come up with one more specific example, detail, or fact that you can add to support the main idea.
- *Five better verbs.* Read through your response, and try to find five weak or vague verbs that could be replaced with stronger, more active ones.
- *Swap out a general noun for a more specific one.* Read through your response, and look for nouns that are vague; replace them with ones that are more

concrete. For example, have you used the word *dog* when you could have painted a more specific, vivid picture by using the word *Doberman*?

- *Read aloud (to yourself)*. Reading aloud is a great revision strategy that just isn't possible in most testing situations, but you can come close. Take your test response, and use another paper or your arm to cover up most of it so that you can read only one line at a time. Mouth the words (silently!) so that you can imagine yourself hearing them aloud. Search for missing words, extra words, and sentences that just feel awkward.

Nora Raleigh Baskin

Nora Raleigh Baskin is the author of eight middle-grades and young-adult novels, including *Anything but Typical* (2009), which won the 2010 American Library Association Schneider Family Book Award, and *The Summer Before Boys* (2011). She teaches creative writing to both adults and children and speaks at schools and libraries around the country. Her Web site is www.norabaskin.com.

I have the same strategy for revision every time. I write the entire novel without looking back. I may get a little feedback from friends with the first twenty to thirty pages before I am really sure of three things: point of view, setting, and tone. Once I have all that I just plow ahead until I am done. Then I print the whole thing out and sit down to read it (and this is important) in one sitting. I hold a pen in my hand, and I mark up the manuscript. Then I input the changes, large and small, and do that whole process again, maybe one more time before letting my editor see it. Then she does the same thing.

TRY IT

Here are the steps for one author-model you might use as a revision strategy.

- Thinking about big-picture revision ideas (don't worry about minor editing yet!), read through your piece of writing from start to finish, making notes in pen or colored pencil.
- Then go back and make changes on your computer document. If it's a handwritten piece, write a new draft with the changes included.
- Read the draft in one sitting, again, and make changes.
- Then give your manuscript to a friend (he or she can play the role of editor) to make notes as well. Remember that writing questions in the margin is a great way to get yourself or another writer thinking about possible changes!

Revision is like a newborn
because it's a 24/7
commitment and worth
every sleepless night.

—KIRBY LARSON

CHAPTER 4

Back to Brainstorming

Sometimes, revision means starting over. Sometimes, a student will write a story or an essay or a research paper, and the focus is all wrong. Maybe the writer drafted a book report when the assignment was a character's diary entry. Maybe he or she tried to focus on too much instead of narrowing down the topic for a research project. There are any number of reasons why starting over with a clean slate might be the best way to approach a revision, but the starting-over kind of revision is also the toughest for kids—and adults—to swallow. Cries of, "I already wrote it once. You want me to write it again?" are understandable. Starting over definitely involves more work, but if you can persuade students that a fresh start still allows them to use the very best of what they've already written, it can go a long way toward easing their pain.

In the winter of 2007–2008, I had just finished a chapter-book manuscript called *Princess Marty Frog Slime and the Nutcracker Ballet*. It was about a girl who liked catching frogs and crayfish, and her parents made her try out for her town's holiday production of *The Nutcracker*. I loved writing this silly story, especially because I'd just finished two regional historical novels set during times of war. I was ready for something light and fun.

I sent the manuscript to my agent, Jennifer. (I've noticed that agents are a lot like teachers in that they talk about doing "your best work" before a story gets sent out to editors.) She read it and sent me a nice e-mail about how much she loved the main character, Marty. But then she asked if the story really had to be about *The Nutcracker* ballet. Couldn't it be about a school play or something universal so kids could relate to it more easily?

My first thought was "Is she serious?" No, the book didn't *have* to be about *The Nutcracker*. I suppose *Moby Dick* didn't really *have* to be about a whale either—but it *was*. And furthermore, I'd be willing to bet that nobody asked Herman Melville if he'd consider telling the story with, say, an octopus or a sheep instead. Did she want me to just start over and rewrite the whole thing? What about all those funny ballet scenes that I liked? I'd worked hard on those!

But somewhere in my whining brain, I heard the echoes of a lot of students I'd taught over the years. What would I say to them? Just try it—and see how it goes.

So I tried it.

First, I made a quick outline of how Marty's story might go if she were forced to be the princess in a school play instead of a ballerina. Then, I went through the manuscript and highlighted all the parts that I might be able to use in the new draft. It turns out there were plenty of things I loved that I could keep. Marty's wildlife-rehabilitator mom got to stay, and so did the animal she was caring for at the time, a rambunctious escape-artist raccoon named Sparky. And of course, Marty was still Marty. She could still love catching frogs and still hate sparkly dresses.

In the end, I had just as much fun drafting that new book as I'd had writing the first one—maybe even more. And when I sent it to Jennifer, she loved it. So did the people at Scholastic who decided that Marty should have her own chapter-book series, and they put the Marty McGuire series on their calendar to debut in May 2011. Starting over wasn't so bad after all.

In fact, ask any published author about big revisions, and you're likely to hear a story about tossing out a draft to begin again.

"Sometimes the entire structure changes—and sometimes the genre," says Tanya Lee Stone, who has written more than eighty books for kids. "I have changed picture books to middle grade, for example, because the story was best served that way." Stone's award-winning nonfiction title *Almost Astronauts* (2009) started as a picture book written in poems about each of the thirteen women who were part of the first program to train women for space. The approach didn't work. "The poems told too little of the story even though they were effective at capturing the essence of each of the women," Stone says. She tried again, and the book went through numerous drafts and forms before she reshaped it into the work of middle-grades/young-adult nonfiction that went on to earn the 2010 Sibert Medal.

Karen Day's first novel, *Tall Tales* (2007), kept getting rejections from publishing houses when her agent first sent it out, but two editors who liked the manuscript asked for revisions. "They both wanted the family to have some 'hope' at the end," Day says. "This was discouraging. I knew that in many alcoholic families the drinker has to hit rock bottom before he/she stops drinking. I stewed over this for weeks. Then an idea came to me. But it would require rewriting the last 100 pages and changing a lot, including the mom's character. I'd never made these kinds of drastic changes before. And so that's what I did."

Day says the process took months, but in the end, both editors made offers to buy the book. "I look back on this a lot and smile. I rewrote 100 pages of my novel and changed a main character's personality all because of one word. *Hope.*"

Deva Fagan encountered a similar challenge when she was working on her second novel, *The Magical Misadventures of Prunella Bogthistle* (2010). She tossed out her entire draft, which had been written in the male main character's point of view, and rewrote it in first person with her female main character narrating. "I did this because both characters came across as flat and cartoony in the first version," Fagan says. "I wish I had tried experimenting earlier on! But sometimes it takes writing a story to realize what isn't working."

Sometimes students need to work out the kinks, too. One of my reluctant student writers had chosen the topic of mandatory helmets for skateboarding as his focus for a persuasive essay. He didn't think kids should have to wear helmets to skate in the local skate park as the city required. Was he going to be able to find facts to support his opinion? Probably not, and I knew this when he shared his topic with me. But I also knew this boy well—he'd have to discover that fact on his own if he was going to take ownership of this piece of writing. Instead of discouraging him, I just nodded, jotted down his topic, and said, "Okay, and understand that we're all just starting our research. So if you end up finding information that changes your mind on this topic, just let me know and you can adjust your thesis."

He spent a class period researching skateboarding injuries and then came back to me. "I can't really find anything that says it's okay for kids not to wear helmets."

"Hmm." I nodded. And waited.

"But I still think it stinks that you can't skate without one. Some kids can't afford helmets. They're expensive."

"So in a perfect world," I said, "how would the city handle this?"

"Well, they could provide helmets for kids who don't have them."

"Great idea!" I sent him back to his computer to rewrite his thesis, and we were both happy when he was able to get back to work. But he had to come to that conclusion on his own, by trying the first idea. We learn a lot from things that don't work out, and this student was able to use many of the notes he took during his original investigation.

When a student's revision would really benefit from the starting-over approach, it's important to emphasize to him or her that the work of that first draft wasn't a waste of time. Some authors even call their first draft their discovery drafts, in which they figure out the story they really want to tell. Then in the second draft—and third and fourth and fifth drafts—they get down to the business of telling it.

But those authors, like those starting-over students, find there's much of that first draft that can be resurrected in the next version, including characters and lines of description and themes. Students will be more likely to give this revision strategy a try if they know that they're not truly starting from square one.

Take Two

What does brainstorming look like when you're starting over? It can take many forms. Most of my "do-over" projects begin that second draft with a page of scribbled notes about what I want to do (see Figure 4.1). That works well for me, whether I'm rewriting a whole book, as I was with *Marty McGuire*, or starting over on a single chapter (which I also did with *Marty McGuire* after I'd rewritten the whole thing!).

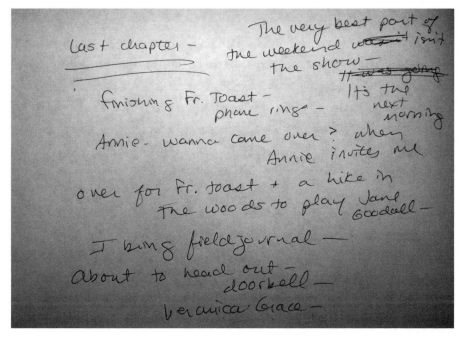

FIGURE 4.1

Revision notes for *Marty McGuire*

Beginnings and endings are important parts of books, so they often need special attention during the revision process. The first and last chapters of my middle-grades novels *The Brilliant Fall of Gianna Z.* and *Sugar and Ice* were all completely rewritten during the revision process with my editor.

When I first sent *The Brilliant Fall of Gianna Z.* to my editor, the book ended with a family scene in the Zales's kitchen. In her revision letter, she asked if I might consider crafting a new ending. "I was also a bit disappointed that we didn't see her run again. Her running is what focuses her and provides stability, and what she worked so hard to be able to participate in. . . . I think it would be great to have her running once more amidst the beautiful scenery that she loves. Perhaps something also leaf-related to pull it all together?"

I found myself nodding as I read this letter from my editor. It was definitely a better way to bring all of the book's threads together—to provide a conclusion that left readers feeling satisfied, too. (I won't spoil it for you by giving too much away.)

New Beginnings

We tell our students how important beginnings and endings are, but how much time do we spend helping them revise these sections of their writing? "Two new beginnings" is a strategy I like to use in my seventh-grade classroom when students have fallen into the trap of boring leads for their essays or reports. When I first started teaching writing, I'd ask my students, "Have you checked to make sure your lead is as strong as it can be?" They'd nod curtly as if they were crossing the idea of revision (and me!) off their lists. These days, I've stopped asking that question. Instead, I review the mini-lesson on writing leads and conclusions. Then we all take time in class to write two new one-paragraph introductions and two new one-paragraph conclusions, using different strategies than in the first draft. After students have completed these new paragraphs, I ask them to read all of their options before choosing the beginning and ending that they really want for their pieces of writing. Inevitably, many choose the new versions—paragraphs they probably never would have written if we hadn't taken the time to try them out in class.

Alexis, for example, had started her personal narrative draft with a conventional opening sentence along the lines of "One of the most exciting moments in my swimming career was . . ." Her brainstorming introductions activity led her to explore some other, more attention-grabbing options, one of which she ended up using as her new beginning. (See Figures 4.2 and 4.3.)

FIGURE 4.2

Alexis tries out new introductions for her personal narrative.

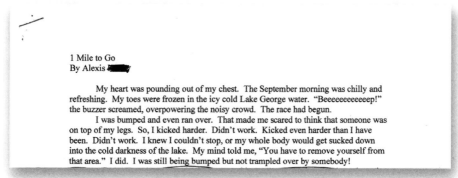

FIGURE 4.3

Alexis's first two paragraphs from the final draft

Like Alexis, my student Breanna played around with a few different introductions before deciding on the one that would ultimately draw readers into
her personal narrative. (See Figures 4.4–4.6.)

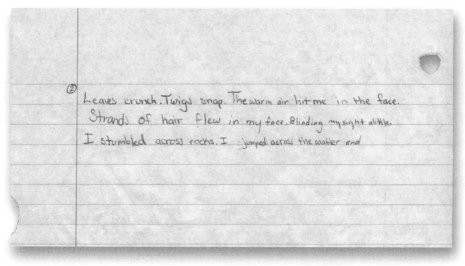

FIGURE 4.4

Breanna's first possible introduction

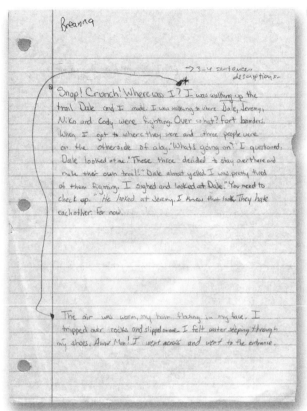

FIGURE 4.5

Breanna's second possible
introduction, with revision notes

Fort Fight!
By: Breanna ████████

    Snap! Crunch! Where was I? The air was warm a little breeze making my hair fly in my face. I tripped and stumble across rocks. I slipped as I jumped across the little old creek. I felt water seeping through my shoes. "Aw man!" I muttered. I wasn't happy. I went through the entrance of the trail that Dale, Niko, Cody and I made. I was walking up to the voices of Dale and Jeremy. Sometimes I could hear Cody butting in. They were fighting. Over what? Fort borders. That's what. When I arrived to where they were, three people were standing on the other side of a rotten log.

    "What's going on?" I question.

    Dale looked at me and answered. "These two decided to stay over on that side of the log and make "there own trail". I don't know about that kid. He just went over there with them," He almost yelled. I was pretty tired of them fighting over stupid stuff. I sighed and looked at Dale, who was looking at Jeremy.

FIGURE 4.6

Breanna's first few paragraphs from the final draft

There are as many different kinds of revision-brainstorming techniques as there are writers. Linda Urban, author of *A Crooked Kind of Perfect* (2007) and *Hound Dog True* (2011), prefers idea webs (see Figure 4.7). "I like certain objects to have a different meaning for different characters in a book," Urban says. "Sometimes I start a web with that object in the center—Popsicles, for example—and then web from there the places that Popsicles occur in the story, the people who eat them or talk about or buy them, and then all the different associations that those people and places have in relation to the Popsicles. Sometimes what I find surprises me. Sometimes it gives me details that I can use in my revision. For one character, I might find that sharing a Popsicle turns out to be a supreme symbol of friendship. For another, it's just a sticky mess on her fingers."

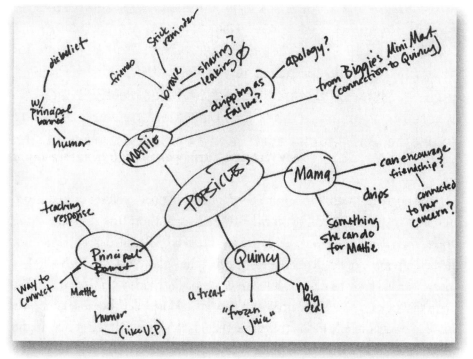

FIGURE 4.7

Linda Urban's Popsicle idea web for *Hound Dog True*

A Tale of Two (or More!) Titles

With titles, I think of what's key in the story. Can it be captured in a concrete item from the story? Or a thought or feeling? Or is there a phrase that gives an idea of what the story is about, especially if it's used in the story? I particularly like double entendres, things that have two meanings that reinforce each other.

—KATHRYN ERSKINE, AUTHOR OF *MOCKINGBIRD*

When I need to brainstorm titles . . . I sit in front of the TV with an 11" by 17" sheet of paper, colored pens, and my old *Roget's Thesaurus*. The senses take in random pictures or words from the TV, the brain tumbles them around, the hand starts taking notes. That's when I tune out the world, focus on what I have, and start thinking more concretely. That's where the thesaurus comes into play. I let one word lead me to another and another as if I'm in a verbal treasure hunt.

—JODY FELDMAN, AUTHOR OF *THE GOLLYWHOPPER GAMES*

You might not realize this, but a good number of books you see on bookstore and library shelves had different titles when their authors first started writing them. *The Brilliant Fall of Gianna Z.* started its life as a book called *Swinger of Birches*, named after one of the Robert Frost poems that play a role in the book. My agent worried that the title might not mean enough to kids who weren't familiar with that poem, so we came up with a new idea—*Maple Girl*, because Gianna is dubbed a sugar maple in the tree game that she and her friend Zig play in the book. Later on in the revision process, my editor wondered if there might be a stronger title, one that did a better job capturing the creative spirit of the book and the humor. So we went back to the drawing board again.

I asked my family for ideas. I asked my seventh-grade students. I asked my editor, my writer pals, my Facebook and Twitter friends, and anyone unlucky enough to run into me on an elevator. There were countless suggestions. They ranged from serious to tongue-in-cheek and included *Catch a Falling Leaf, The Leaf Game, Cookie Crumbs in the Coffins* (Gianna's grandmother brings her famous "funeral cookies" to all the wakes in the family's funeral home), and (my favorite) *That Stupid Leaf Book*. Finally, a combination of ideas came together to make *The Brilliant Fall of Gianna Z.*, which we thought captured the spirit of the book.

The same thing happened with *Sugar and Ice*, my figure-skating novel for middle-grades readers. It was originally called *Sugar on Snow*, named for the sweet maple treat the main character's family serves on their maple farm. But again, an e-mail arrived from my editor, wondering if there might be a stronger title, one that let readers know this was a skating book. Again, we started brainstorming and tossed dozens of titles around, but none of them seemed just right.

I'm a big fan of magnetic poetry. I love the way moving words around physically leads to unexpected combinations. Could a strategy like that help with my title? It was worth a shot. One night at my kitchen table, I made a list of all the possible titles that had already been discussed, as well as a list of words that had to do with skating, ice rinks, and maple farms. Then I cut up the list so that each word was on its own slip of paper. I slid the words around and wrote down possible combinations. I even threw them up in the air a few times to see what words landed near one another, just in case a random landing would produce the right combination. (See Figure 4.8.)

FIGURE 4.8

Brainstorming a title for *Sugar and Ice*

At the end of this exercise, I sent a new list to my editor, and after much discussion, we decided that *Sugar and Ice* was the right title for this story—sweet but cold, capturing both the main character's personality and the challenge of competing with some hard-edged skaters in her new training situation in Lake Placid.

The paper-and-scissors method is a great one to use in the classroom, too. Students can brainstorm words and phrases that relate to their writing, cut up the paper so there's one word per slip, and rearrange and jot down possibilities. Have more wall space than table space? Use sticky notes instead of regular paper, and students can rearrange words to make titles on the classroom or hallway walls.

This is one of those activities that won't lend itself to a quiet classroom day, so be ready for that, and take advantage of it. Talking, after all, is a powerful form of brainstorming.

If you don't have time or materials handy for the paper-and-scissors title strategy, try this one. I call it "Ten Terrific Titles," and here's what I tell students who are having title stress:

Get a piece of paper and force yourself to write down ten possible titles for your piece of writing. You have to come up with ten. Write fast. It doesn't matter how stupid or boring you think the titles might be; write them down. And keep writing. When you finish, take a look at your list, and one of those titles will be waving at you. "Me!" it'll say. "I'm the title you wanted!" Write it at the top of your page, and you're done.

Danette Haworth

Danette Haworth is the author of *Violet Raines Almost Got Struck by Lightning* (2008), *The Summer of Moonlight Secrets* (2010), and *Me and Jack* (2011). Growing up in a military family, Danette lived up and down the East Coast and in Turkey and England; she now calls Orlando, Florida, her home. Visit her online at www.danettehaworth.com.

I worked on my first book under the title **Crossing the Econlockhatchee** *Bridge. This working title was functional in that the story is literally and metaphorically about crossing a bridge. But every time I saw that title in the header of my draft, I felt disappointed by it. No color, no fun, no personality! Using a pen and paper, I brainstormed keywords taken directly from the draft. I thought about concepts and the feeling and rhythm of the words. For some reason, long titles with character names appeal to me, so I tried to come up with something along those lines. Once I put Violet's name into the title, the rest fell easily into place; almost getting struck by lightning is a pivotal event in Violet's life. The new title,* **Violet Raines Almost Got Struck by Lightning,** *conveyed a sense of Violet's character. The kind of girl who almost gets struck by lightning is not a sit-around type. She's exciting!*

The Summer of Moonlight Secrets was originally titled **The Hotel of Blueberry Goodness,** *but as the book took on a mysterious slant, my editor and I realized that even though we loved Blueberry Goodness, it no longer fit. The main elements and characters from the proposal were there and, for the most part, they were very close to their original descriptions. But it was somehow a different story; the original title didn't fit anymore. My editor, Stacy, and I e-mailed back and forth, each of us hammering out keywords or phrases we thought depicted the book. We made*

long lists, commented on each other's suggestions, explaining why we thought certain words worked and why other words didn't. The title has a big burden—it has to convey the attitude and nature of the story in just a few words. We agreed we wanted it to whisper with mystery; it had to be summery, and it couldn't sound ominous or supernatural. So we had to step back and think about what this story was really about. Much of the story takes place in hidden rooms and forgotten passageways—we knew secrets were important, and moonlight, too, since the more mysterious elements take place at night. Summer was key in all that summer conveys—freedom; friends; long, hot days; late nights; and new adventures. After a flurry of exchanges between Stacy and me, and a meeting at Walker, the new title emerged: **The Summer of Moonlight Secrets.**

TRY IT

Need a title for your piece of writing? Try to go beyond the obvious by brainstorming in the table below. In each box, write one word that has to do with your story or report. Like Danette Haworth, you'll want to choose the most vivid words that really capture the feeling of what you wrote. Then use a pair of scissors to cut the table so each word is on its own piece of paper. Experiment by moving the pieces around to come up with different combinations. When you finish, you will have a whole new list of title possibilities!

TITLE-TALK BRAINSTORMING TABLE

Kathi Appelt

Kathi Appelt is the author of more than thirty-five books for children and young adults. Most recently, she has written two middle-grades novels: Newbery Honor and NBA finalist *The Underneath* (2008) and *Keeper* (2010). She lives in College Station, Texas, with her husband, Ken, and four cats. Her Web site is www.kathiappelt.com.

I keep a "project journal" for each book that I'm working on, and I use that journal as a kind of dialogue between myself and the story. Most of the pages in that journal start with the two syllables "what if . . ." and go from there. In the journal I draw maps and free-write about the characters and where they're going. I ask all sorts of questions, and then I try to answer them.

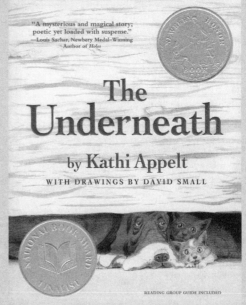

TRY IT

Try Kathi Appelt's "what-if" strategy to explore some possibilities that might take you in new directions as you revise. Use the space below to come up with at least three "what-if" questions. What if my main character decided to drop out of the spelling bee? What if she gets in trouble on that day, on purpose? Ask those kinds of questions—and then answer them. Ready . . . go!

What if _____?

My answer: If that happened, then

What if _____?

My answer: If that happened, then

What if _____?

My answer: If that happened, then

Erin Dionne

Erin Dionne is a writer, an editor, and a college professor with an MFA in creative writing from Emerson College. Erin lives outside of Boston with her family and dog, Grafton. Her first novel, *Models Don't Eat Chocolate Cookies* (2009), was selected as a Featured Title for Scholastic Book Fairs, and an early version of the *Models* manuscript (titled *Beauty Binge*) was named as one of PEN/New England's 2006 Susan P. Bloom Discovery Night Award winners. Erin's Web site can be found at www.erindionne.com.

For every project that I start, I brainstorm in a notebook. I make a lot of arrows and lists. I do bubble diagrams. I do that at first when I'm just starting to get to know my character and where my story is going to go. Then when I get stuck, this is the place that I go back to. I go back and reread the notes that I've already taken, and then I go back and I brainstorm again.

TRY IT

One of the lists in Erin Dionne's notebook was a character love/hate chart that she'd created for her forthcoming novel, *Notes from an Accidental Band Geek*. It helped her explore her main character Elsie's personality by examining the things Elsie loved and hated the most.

What does your character love more than anything? What's at the top of your character's "Hate" list? Use the chart below to brainstorm.

Character's Name_____

Loves	Hates

Revision is like doing a
puzzle because it feels so
good when you snap that
last piece in.

—DANETTE HAWORTH

CHAPTER 5

Real Authors Don't Plan . . . Or Do They?

I'd been working on a new writing project, a mystery for middle-grades readers, for several months when I got an e-mail from my friend Penny Smith, a fifth-grade teacher in upstate New York. One of her students, Tyler, was fighting her efforts to teach the planning stage of the writing process. "Real writers don't plan," he told her. "They just write whatever comes into their heads."

Penny wondered if I might be able to respond to her note and give Tyler a more complete picture of how "real writers" work. Her timing in sending the note couldn't have been better. The book I was writing had been getting the best of me for a few weeks. I'd started writing—then stopped, started and stopped again, taken a break to travel to Washington, D.C., for the research I was sure would be the answer to everything, and then started and stopped again. I'd recently come to the conclusion that what I really needed was to stop writing and revise with the help of a better road map. I needed a plan.

After reading some resources about how to plot mysteries, brainstorming the time line, and outlining the sequence of events, I was able to get back to work and finish the book. Here's the letter I wrote to Penny (and Tyler), which I published on my blog:

Dear Tyler,

So I heard a rumor today. Is it true that you told your teacher that real authors don't use story webs or outlines or plan their writing? That real authors just write whatever comes into their heads and if they need to outline or do any prep work, they're not real writers?

Hmm.

Your teacher dropped me a note to ask if I might be able to make you reconsider. She's a friend of mine and knows that I've written eight books for kids—three that are out now and five that will be published in 2010 and 2011. And she has a pretty good idea what "real writing" looks like.

I told her I'd share some photos tonight, because I thought you might like to see some of the planning I do (see Figure 5.1).

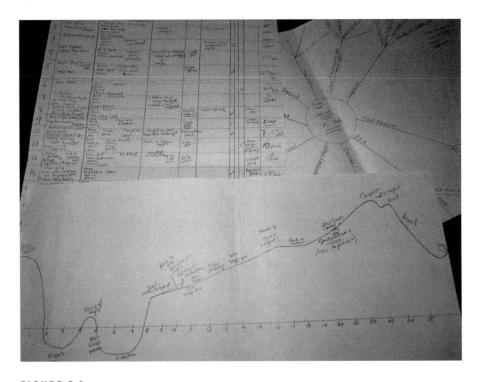

FIGURE 5.1

A collection of planning pages used in the writing of *The Star Spangled Setup*

This is some of the prewriting I've done for the book I'm writing right now. It's a middle-grades mystery, and I'm finished with my draft, but I'll be revising for a while now, trying to make it better. What you're looking at in the photo includes the following:

- A time line showing where all the characters are throughout the story and what happens when (top left)
- Page two of the time line (top middle)
- A list of things I needed to research (top right)
- A character brainstorming chart with notes on the three kids' personalities, interests, families, etc. (middle left)
- A story web showing how the central mystery relates to the clues, villains, setting, etc. (middle right)
- A plot diagram that I did to make sure the story gets more exciting as it goes along, right up to the climax (bottom left)
- A chapter-by-chapter outline of characters, action, settings, plot threads, and theme connections (bottom center)
- A chart listing secondary characters hanging around the airport where the story is set and their stories (bottom right)

And then there's my revision to-do list, with jobs for each chapter (see Figure 5.2). I'm on Chapter 13 right now.

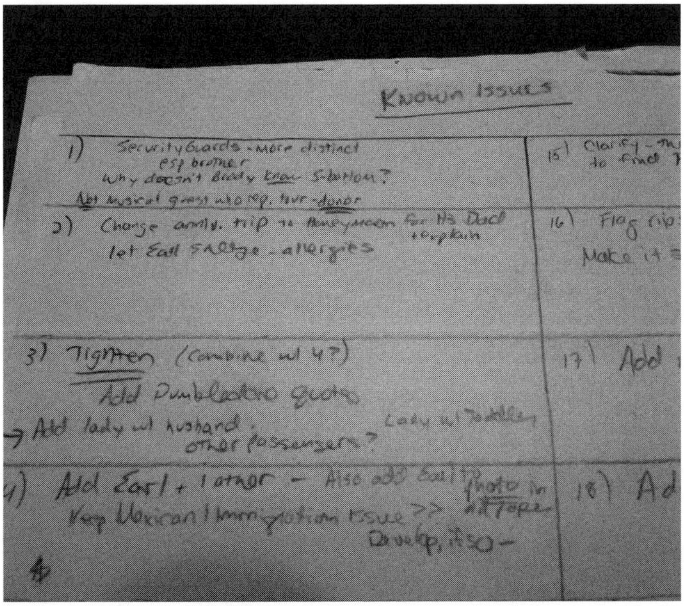

FIGURE 5.2

Revision to-do list for *The Star Spangled Setup*

So do I do all this stuff for every novel I write? Nope. But I use a lot of it with each book.

And do I always outline and plan before I write? Well, your teacher might not like this, but no. Sometimes I just plunge in and write for a little while. That kind of freewriting can help you get good ideas, but it's also scattered and unorganized and hard for readers to follow, so even if I start a book by freewriting, I usually don't make it all the way through. Once I have an idea where the story is going, I stop and—you guessed it—make an outline, a road map that can get me to the end.

Having practice with a lot of different kinds of brainstorming, story mapping, and outlining helps me make sure I have the skills I need to write whatever I want to write. It's like having a big toolbox. You might not need the hammer for every single project, but you'd sure be lost without it, and if you have one, you can pull it out whenever you need it.

So give the outline a try, okay? Real writers do use the tools your teacher is talking about, and we use them all the time.

I hope your fantasy story turns out beautifully.

All the best,

Kate Messner

P.S. I am sorry about this post. I used to hate it when my teachers were right about things like this . . .

Organized for Success

So you see, real writers do plan at different stages of the writing process, including revision. What kind of planning tools are best? It depends on what kind of revision problem the writer is trying to solve. For example, when I was sorting out the mystery elements for *The Star Spangled Setup*, the first in my Silver Jaguar Society mystery series with Scholastic due out in 2012, I really needed a specialized graphic organizer that focused on the ingredients for a mystery: the suspect, clues, motives, false leads, investigators, and red herrings. (See Figure 5.3.)

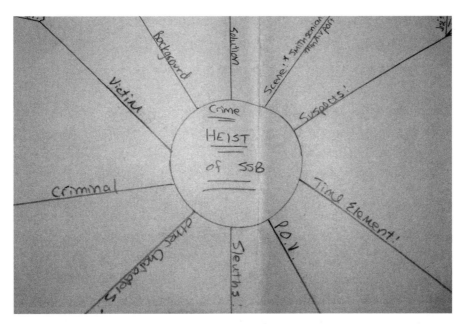

FIGURE 5.3

A story web of mystery elements used in the planning of *The Star Spangled Setup*

It was a different story when I was working on Draft 7 of my figure-skating novel, *Sugar and Ice*. One of the copyeditors noticed that the time line seemed to be off. In fact, I seem to have waved a magic writer wand and turned a Monday into a Wednesday in the middle of a chapter. Which day, she wondered, did I mean for it to be?

Which day? Monday, of course! The day before had been Sunday, and the main character had returned to training. Except when I reread the chapter, I realized that there were certain reasons why it had to be a Wednesday.

To straighten things out, I had to use a different kind of planning tool—a good, old-fashioned calendar. I went online and found calendars for the months of March through December, the time period covered in the novel. I went through chapter by chapter and marked on the calendar which pages covered which days, what was happening each week in terms of the main character's growth as a skater, and when her competitions occurred. This calendar-planning revision strategy helped me clean up the Monday-Wednesday snafu and alerted me to some other minor timing errors that we were able to fix before the final printing.

Lisa Schroeder, author of *It's Raining Cupcakes* (2010), is a fan of calendars during the revision process, too. "I use calendars all the time in both my writing and revision process, because it's important to keep track of days, what holidays might fall around the time period, what the weather might be like, and other seasonal things like food or plants that might or might not be available," Schroeder says. "Keeping a calendar really helps the time period I'm writing about feel more real."

To Plan or Not to Plan?

Often, when I visit classrooms to talk about my books, students will ask me about planning. "Do you always write an outline before you start writing a book?" When I answer, "No, not always," at least one student looks smugly at his or her teacher, and I can only imagine the arguments about process that must have preceded that question. But the truth is the truth; I sometimes have an idea for a book, an idea that lives in my brain and travels around with me through many days of teaching and driving my kids to sports practices. When I'm ready to start writing, I sometimes plunge in without planning. However, I do find that after I have a sense for the voice of a project, once I'm warmed up, I need to step back from that fast-track writing to plan.

Usually, the projects that start with a plunge instead of a plan require me to stop along the way and backtrack. I'll realize halfway through, for example, that the main character's goal has changed or that I don't really know where the stolen goods are hidden, and that's where planning as a revision strategy really comes in. At this stage, I appreciate having a wide variety of planning strategies in my writer's toolbox.

When my seventh-grade students resist planning at the beginning of a writing project, I often ask them a few questions: What's the focus of your writing going to be? Do you know how you want to start? Do you have a sense for where the piece is heading?

If students have some sense of direction and are eager to get writing, I might let them skip the planning part of the process, at least for the time being. Some student writers, like some adult authors, simply feel better diving into a story, and I don't like to get in the way of what may be a perfectly viable process just because that process might be different from what I learned in teacher school.

A Medley of Methods

Planning is important, but sometimes it doesn't have to come first. The revision strategies talked about in this chapter can help students who find they need to return to this part of the process, or visit it for the first time, while revising.

OUTLINING

Outlines are very useful to me after I write. It's a way of laying out what I've got, sort of like a bunch of puzzle pieces, and trying to fit them all together.

—KATHRYN ERSKINE, AUTHOR OF *MOCKINGBIRD*

For Loree Griffin Burns, author of nonfiction titles such as *Tracking Trash* (2007) and *The Hive Detectives* (2010), planning means looking not only at the content of the book but also at the structure. Reading like a writer—looking at other texts with an eye for what works well—helps her discover the best way to organize her own ideas. "I pay close attention to the structures of the books I am reading all the time, and I compare and contrast it to the structure I'm working with," Burns says. "This is always helpful to me, because it gives me confidence . . . or, in some cases, helps me see why my own structure is not working."

As for traditional outlining, ask a hundred authors their thoughts, and you're likely to get a hundred different answers.

Nora Raleigh Baskin, author of *All We Know of Love* (2008) and *Anything but Typical* (2009), says she never outlines because that's just not how her creative process works. "But when I wrote *All We Know of Love*, which takes place on a bus ride, I had to figure out my times and locations more specifically," she says. "To be honest, I wrote the whole story and then went back and made the times and locations fit. I looked up bus schedules and stations and weather reports and maps from Connecticut to Florida, and when I needed to, I made the bus break down."

Kathi Appelt, author of *The Underneath* (2008) and *Keeper* (2010), would rather know where she's going from the beginning of the trip. "I like having a road map," Appelt says. "I'm happiest when I know how a story ends fairly quickly in the process. It's like knowing your destination when you get in the car. I stop constantly to adjust, rethink, etc. Time lines do help me, but I usually don't discover them until late in the process, and then I use them to 'test' the story, to make sure that my time frame makes logical sense."

TIME LINES

I often spread out along the entire dining room table with a kind of time line of the book to see whether the story has the right kind of flow I am looking for.

—TANYA LEE STONE, AUTHOR OF *ALMOST ASTRONAUTS*

A time line can help writers of any age keep track of what's happening with different story threads, or in different locations, at the same time. I created the time line in Figure 5.4 to help keep track of characters and plot threads in my mystery, *The Star Spangled Setup*. The book takes place over just twenty-four hours, so it was important for me to know where all the characters were during those hours. The bad guys needed time to hide evidence, and my twelve-year-old protagonists had to check in with their parents every few hours as they investigated the crime.

In this case, a time line helped me to make sure the plot of this mystery was plausible, that people had the time to get from place to place and accomplish what needed to be done. (This time line, by the way, is a great example of why I'm not a fan of grading student planning papers. It's messy and probably doesn't make much sense at all to you. However, as the author of this piece, I understand it just fine, and it accomplished exactly what I needed it to do. Student planning pages don't necessarily need to be perfectly clear to the whole world either. They just need to serve as road maps for the writers.)

Time lines can also be invaluable when students are writing nonfiction. A student writing a research paper about the American Revolution, for example, will get a much broader perspective on the war and any individual event within it by creating a time line that shows what battles and milestones occurred, where they occurred, and how those events are interconnected.

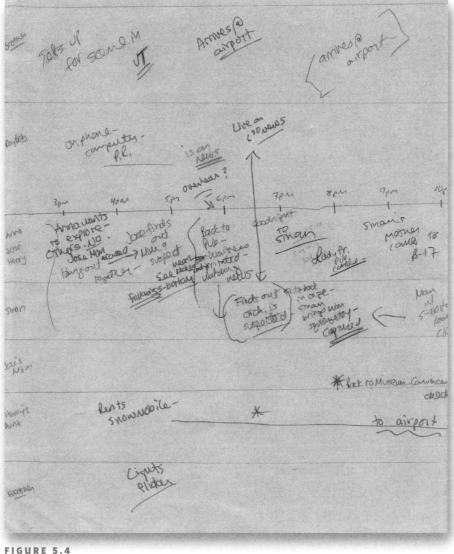

FIGURE 5.4

A time line follows characters through *The Star Spangled Setup*.

LISTS AND SPREADSHEETS

After the first draft, when I have the basic shape of my story, I create a list of the characters and their attributes. If I didn't do this, I'd have no idea who has green eyes and who has brown hair. I also make a map of the world I've created and a time line chart. I've caught many mistakes after making the time line chart—like missing days or having a full moon one night and a full moon again the next week. Readers will catch your mistakes, believe me.

—SUZANNE SELFORS, AUTHOR OF *SMELLS LIKE DOG*

I have a spreadsheet I developed to map out my book chapter by chapter. It delineates page numbers, pertinent plot issues, and characters who appear. It really helps me see when characters drop out for too long or disappear altogether.

—ERIC LUPER, AUTHOR OF *JEREMY BENDER VS. THE CUPCAKE CADETS*

Lists and spreadsheets are also helpful tools when the revision process takes a writer back to the planning stage. They help writers with consistency and pacing. A spreadsheet view can quickly alert an author when a character or plot thread has dropped out of the story for too long, and lists are great reminders of character traits and overall rules of the story's world.

INDEX CARDS

For both *The Gollywhopper Games* and *The Seventh Level*, I also made a set of index cards—one card per scene—then dealt them out in a different order to see what might happen if some of the scenes exchanged places.

—JODY FELDMAN, AUTHOR OF *THE GOLLYWHOPPER GAMES* AND *THE SEVENTH LEVEL*

Lately I've been planning more during the initial stages of writing because of a software program called Scrivener, a word-processing and planning tool for writers that's available for Mac and PC computers. I love this program. In fact, I've become sort of a self-proclaimed "Scrivenevangelist," touting the joys of the planning-drafting blend. My favorite part of the program is the index-card feature, which enables me to plan my chapters quickly (great for someone who doesn't like to plan ahead) as I write my chapters and scenes. Scrivener puts each of my scene titles on a little index card that appears to be pinned to a bulletin board. I can drag the cards around to rearrange scenes, and all the text from that file goes with them. I can even color code the cards so I know, for example, just how many of my scenes take place at a certain setting or with certain characters in the spotlight. (See Figures 5.5 and 5.6.)

FIGURE 5.5

A Scrivener revision session at the kitchen table

FIGURE 5.6

Scrivener's index-card/corkboard feature

Your students will probably love Scrivener, too, but if computer availability and software budgets won't accommodate its use, you can recreate the cool index-card feature on a classroom table or floor.

My teaching colleague Marjorie Light and I used this strategy with our advanced creative writing class about halfway through the semester. Our students had developed their basic premises and characters and started their stories, but many didn't have a clear picture of where they were going. We passed out index cards and colored pencils and asked the students to read through their manuscripts and make a list of the major scenes, with one scene title on each index card. Then we asked them to project the next few scenes and add those ideas to new cards. You can plan an entire novel this way. This revision strategy has proven to be a useful one for cleaning up dead-end plot points and getting writers who are stuck moving again.

Index cards have long been a staple of the traditional research project, but color coding can lead to more effective revision strategies here, too. Students can color code their note cards based on main ideas, paper clip them together, and rearrange whole paragraphs this way to find the most effective way to present information. Are some color-coded piles lighter than others? That can send a very clear and tactile message to students that a return to research might be necessary in order to fully develop all aspects of the project.

Perhaps the greatest beauty of those index cards is that they can be moved around, rearranged, and plucked out of the lineup to see what the story or report might be like another way. Imagining the maybes is a big part of the revision process.

Should student writers have the same options in terms of when and how they choose to plan? Perhaps if we introduce the idea of planning and outlining as revision activities, rather than something that must be done up front, we'll provide new options and win over some of those reluctant planners.

Each year, for example, my seventh graders complete a piece of persuasive writing in which they research and use their findings to support a position. The International Reading Association's ReadWriteThink Web site (http://www.readwritethink.org) has a great, interactive planning tool for persuasive writing that I demonstrate at the beginning of our unit. I invite my students to use it when planning their writing or to do some freewriting on their topic first and return to the planning tool later. Used as a revision tool in this way, the planner actually helps students discover the gaps in their logic and the missing pieces in their arguments.

In the spring of 2010, I was teaching a unit on persuasive writing just after the BP oil spill in the Gulf of Mexico, and many of my students chose to write letters on this topic, urging the government to take stronger action to solve the problem. Creating a planning map using the ReadWriteThink tool allowed them to clarify their arguments. What specifically did they want to happen? More funding for cleanup? Legal action taken against the company responsible for the spill? It also allowed them to separate their emotional response to the situation from the actual facts they had collected to support their opinions. Some realized as they filled out the planning page that their initial research had focused only on wildlife affected by the oil spill, and they realized they needed to go back to the library to gather more information about the human and economic impacts, too.

Students' topics ranged from global environmental issues to more localized ones, such as the letter Katie wrote to the school principal about gum chewing. This, too, required evidence to support her argument, and Katie's planning page in Figure 5.7 shows how she organized her thoughts.

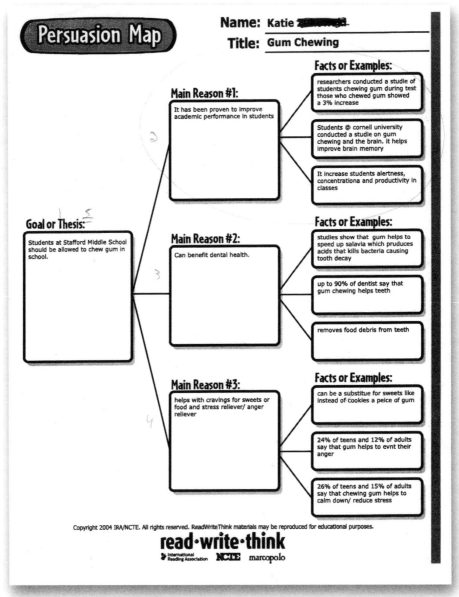

Persuasion Map

Name: Katie ~~Zimmerman~~

Title: Gum Chewing

Goal or Thesis:

Students at Stafford Middle School should be allowed to chew gum in school.

Main Reason #1:

It has been proven to improve academic performance in students

Facts or Examples:

researchers conducted a studie of students chewing gum during test those who chewed gum showed a 3% increase

Students @ cornell university conducted a studie on gum chewing and the brain. it helps improve brain memory

It increase students alertness, concentrationa and productivity in classes

Main Reason #2:

Can benefit dental health.

Facts or Examples:

studies show that gum helps to speed up salavia which pruduces acids that kills bacteria causing tooth decay

up to 90% of dentist say that gum chewing helps teeth

removes food debris from teeth

Main Reason #3:

helps with cravings for sweets or food and stress reliever/ anger reliever

Facts or Examples:

can be a substitue for sweets like instead of cookies a peice of gum

24% of teens and 12% of adults say that gum helps to evnt their anger

26% of teens and 15% of adults say that chewing gum helps to calm down/ reduce stress

read·write·think

International Reading Association   NCTE   marcopolo

FIGURE 5.7

Katie used the ReadWriteThink planning page to gather evidence to support her letter to our school principal.

When we give student writers easy and visual methods of revising their writing we open the door to expanded thinking and creative possibilities.

Nan Marino

Nan Marino, an author and a librarian, lives at the New Jersey shore with her husband and their very large dog. When she isn't working in a library or writing middle-grades stories, Nan hangs out in bookstores or daydreams near the Barnegat Bay. Her debut novel, *Neil Armstrong Is My Uncle & Other Lies Muscle Man McGinty Told Me* (2009), was named an SCBWI Golden Kite Honor Recipient. Her Web site is www.nanmarino.com.

*In **Neil Armstrong Is My Uncle**, the events revolved around the first moon walk. I had a calendar of 1969 (which also included the phases of the moon) to make sure that I got it right. I also created a map of Ramble Street so I knew where everyone's house was. It's a good thing, too. I noticed in one of the final drafts that one character's house was on both ends of the block.*

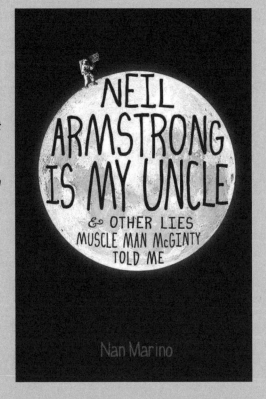

TRY IT

Get a big, blank piece of paper and some colored pencils and create a map that shows where your piece of writing takes place. Is it a neighborhood? Think about the streets and houses, yards and shortcuts. Is it a fantasy world? You'll need to decide where the lakes, rivers, and mountains are. Once you have the basic world of your piece of writing down on the map, you can start to sketch in little drawings and notes about where important events take place.

Use this strategy for works of nonfiction, too. For research papers about historical events, make a map of the area where the event takes place, and pencil in notes about where the action happened. And understand that maps aren't limited to geographic locations; you can also "map" the human digestive system, a cell, the water cycle, or the layers of the atmosphere as a way to clarify your ideas for informational writing.

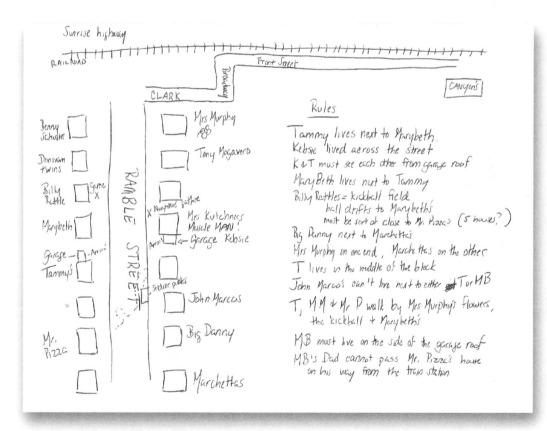

Revision is like carving a
path through a corn maze.
Hard work but so much
fun results.

—ROSE KENT

CHAPTER 6

Big-Picture Revision

I can say with 100 percent certainty that writing for publication has made me a better teacher, but not for the reasons you might think.

Sure, I study the craft of writing, read good books, and figure out what makes them tick. And, yes, it's nice that my name is on some books in the school library; it helps with the credibility factor. But the number-one reason writing has made me a better teacher? Empathy.

When one of my students crosses his or her arms, slouches down in a chair, and scowls at a piece of writing that needs more work, I get it. Revising a novel is wonderful because it's such a long piece of writing; when you get stuck, you can always trot off to another part of the book and work on that. But revising a novel is also a nightmare because it's such a long piece of writing. There can be a feeling of never being finished, and sometimes it's tough to see the whole thing at once.

Even shorter pieces of writing can feel this way to our students, which might be one of the reasons they immediately start looking for the spell-check function when we talk about revision. Spell-check is simple. It's quick. It's manageable. And they know how to do it. It's also not real revision—it's window dressing.

How can we help students look at big-picture revision issues? We can start by talking about what some of those issues might be.

Theme

When I'm revising one of my novels for young readers, I ask myself one question over and over again: What is this piece *really* about? With *The Brilliant Fall of Gianna*

Z., the answer to that question was twofold: the book is about finding your own way to be successful in a world that throws you a lot of curveballs. It's also about the strength we find in family, friends, and creativity. *Sugar and Ice* is about finding the strength to choose your own dreams instead of following a path that might seem to be laid out for you.

Asking that question repeatedly—What is this piece *really* about?—always helps me through the revision process because I can decide what to work on, what to keep or delete, and what to develop more thoroughly.

One of the ways we can frame this revision stage for students is by reconsidering the theme of a piece of writing. While we often think of theme as it relates to fiction, this question is important for works of nonfiction as well. In a persuasive essay, that theme is the thesis statement, the argument that everything in the essay needs to support. In a research paper, it's the particular target idea. Student research projects tend to be strongest when they focus on a theme. Instead of writing in general terms about the American Revolution in Boston, for example, a student might focus on why Boston was a hotbed for Revolutionary activity. This theme, or focus, helps students revise more efficiently whether their project is a persuasive essay, a report, or a story.

"Often the theme I thought I was writing about isn't actually the theme I end up with," says author Deva Fagan. "For example, I'm revising a book right now that I thought was about how you change the world, but is really about the price of secrets. So now I'm using that theme to shape my revision—cutting scenes that don't have to do with secrets, and reshaping others to focus on the characters dealing with various secrets they have to conceal or reveal."

Author Linda Urban says she often discovers the true theme of her book as she's finishing the first draft and looks to strengthen it during the revision process. "Let's say that one of the themes of the book is power—who has it, who doesn't, how to get it, how to recognize it," Urban says. "I can look back at a scene of two characters talking and change small details to underscore that theme. What if one of them did something as simple as absentmindedly switching on and off a flashlight as they talk? What would that say about who was in control? How might it underscore the idea of power? How might the other character's reaction tell us something about how powerful or weak she feels in the situation? It's a little thing, but I'm a big believer in the mighty work that small details can accomplish."

In poetry, looking at the big-picture revision means figuring out the goal of the poem and whether that goal has been met through the use of details and specific words.

"I read the poem . . . to make sure that it makes sense—that it conveys what it was intended to convey, whether it's a story or an emotion or an image," says poet Kelly Fineman. "Sometimes this is not the case, and I've seized on a completely wrong word, phrase, or image during construction. If that's the case, I replace the wrong word(s), let the poem sit again, and come back to it later."

Author Sarah Albee likes to remind herself of the big-picture revision issues by creating a mission statement for every book she writes. "I tape it up near my computer and try to stay true to it," she says. "After I finish a draft, I do a search-and-destroy and cut stuff that isn't relevant."

Students can use a similar process in the classroom. When they complete a rough draft, I'll sometimes ask them to do a little journaling to jump-start the revision process later on. Here are some prompts that have helped my students think about big-picture revision issues:

- What is this piece of writing supposed to do? (inform, persuade, entertain?)
- What is this piece of writing really about?
- Summarize your writing in one sentence.
- If your paper could talk back to you, what would it say is missing?
- If this were someone else's paper, what questions would you ask about it?
- What are the best and worst things about this paper?

Once students know what their writing is about—what its job is supposed to be—they can begin to get rid of elements that don't serve that purpose and develop elements that do. One of the best ways to encourage deep revision is to discourage what I call "surface stuff" until the end of the process. I don't want my students worrying about the correct spelling of words in paragraphs that might end up getting cut anyway.

Seeing the Forest Instead of the Trees

For whatever reason, bright colors help me when I'm revising a novel. I make use of a technique that author Darcy Pattison (2010) has dubbed the "shrunken manuscript," which allows me to see the big picture in a way that's tough to get with full-length novels. The strategy involves single-spacing a manuscript, making the margins as small as my printer will allow, and then shrinking the type to size 8 font, the smallest I can still read. This condenses my 200-page manuscript to thirty to fifty pages, which I can deal out on the floor of my sunroom like a deck of cards (see Figure 6.1).

FIGURE 6.1

The Brilliant Fall of Gianna Z. getting the "shrunken manuscript" treatment

With the whole book laid out in front of me, I bring out the sticky notes. I love these things so much, I should buy stock in a sticky-note company. I assign a label to each color, depending on which big-picture revision issue I want to address. It might be a character I want to make sure is represented through the whole book or a particular plot element I want to recur. For this revision of *The Brilliant Fall of Gianna Z.*, the pink sticky notes represent major plot points—important things happening that move the story forward.

The orange notes mark places where Gianna's funny little brother Ian is in the story; I used these to make sure there was plenty of humor. The green notes represent Gianna's changing relationship with her best guy friend, Zig, to help me make sure I was letting that relationship change and grow the way it should. The blue notes represent Ruby, a girl who started out as a minor character but became more important after my first draft. And the yellow notes mark places where my characters played the leaf game, a fun little game where they decide what kind of tree a person would be. (See Figure 6.2.)

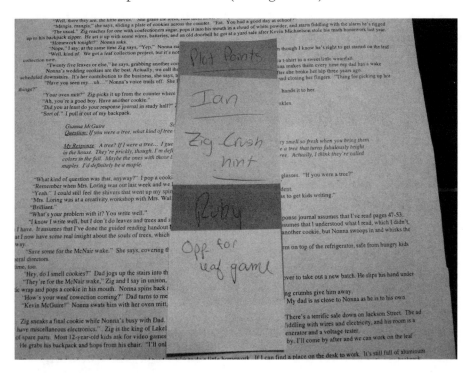

FIGURE 6.2
What the sticky notes mean

With the colored labels arranged like ornaments on a Christmas tree, I could step back and see the whole book. Too few orange notes? Maybe things were getting too serious and I should bring Ian into one of those scenes. When I found several pages without a pink note, I realized that the story needed to move along more quickly; time to trim. Too many pages without a yellow note? I got back down on the floor to read, searching for a place within those pages where the leaf game could come into play.

Even with a much smaller-scale project, students can use a similar color-coding activity to get a new view of their writing. When my students started revising their persuasive essays, they used a colored-pencil activity to "see" what they had already written (see Figures 6.3 and 6.4). Here are the directions:

- Underline your thesis statement—the main argument of your essay—in red.
- What are the reasons you gave for people to support your thesis? These should be the main ideas of your body paragraphs. Underline them in yellow.
- Find facts and details from your research that support your main ideas. Underline these in blue.
- Find sentences that serve to explain and expand on the facts and details. Underline these in green.

FIGURE 6.3
Dallas evaluates his persuasive writing using the color-coding strategy.

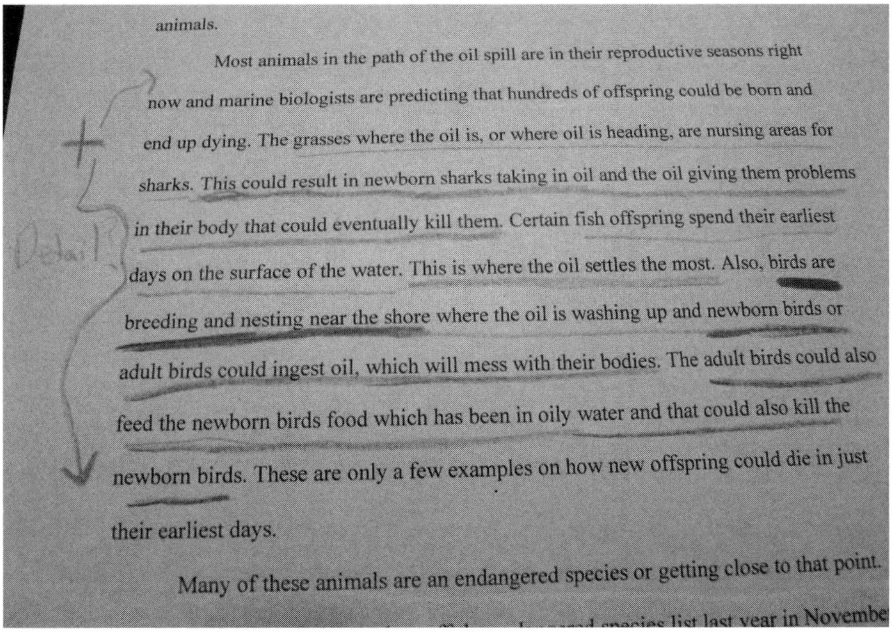

animals.

Most animals in the path of the oil spill are in their reproductive seasons right now and marine biologists are predicting that hundreds of offspring could be born and end up dying. The grasses where the oil is, or where oil is heading, are nursing areas for sharks. This could result in newborn sharks taking in oil and the oil giving them problems in their body that could eventually kill them. Certain fish offspring spend their earliest days on the surface of the water. This is where the oil settles the most. Also, birds are breeding and nesting near the shore where the oil is washing up and newborn birds or adult birds could ingest oil, which will mess with their bodies. The adult birds could also feed the newborn birds food which has been in oily water and that could also kill the newborn birds. These are only a few examples on how new offspring could die in just their earliest days.

Many of these animals are an endangered species or getting close to that point.

FIGURE 6.4

Another student paper, after color coding to identify important elements

As students underline, they begin to notice things.

"I'm pretty sure I waited too long to share my thesis statement."

"I don't have enough supporting details in my third paragraph."

"There's no green on my paper. I think maybe I need to elaborate more."

"Hey, wait! I don't think I even *have* a thesis statement."

This activity is one of my favorites for jump-starting the revision process, and it can be adapted for almost any kind of writing. Just choose three or more things that are important to that particular piece and assign each one a color. For short stories, you might ask students to underline setting details in one color, character development in another, dialogue in a third, and so on. For poetry with an emphasis on sensory language, for example, you might assign one color to the sense of sight, one to smell, one to hearing, one to touch, and one to taste, so that students can identify whether or not they've appealed to all five senses. For poetry with an emphasis on poetic devices, you might ask students to find the similes, metaphors, alliteration, and personification.

Research papers in content-area subjects can also benefit from color-coding activities. Sometimes, when students are completing a report for science or social studies, their writing reads more like a list of notes taken from encyclopedia articles than an actual report. Informational pieces need to contain a blend of topic sentences, details from student research, explanation and clarification, and transitions from one main idea to the next. Identifying these elements by color coding a draft can help students figure out what's missing and prompt them to add what's needed to bring voice, clarity, and smoother transitions to informational writing.

The possibilities are endless, and this strategy really helps students focus on particular aspects of good writing, no matter the genre.

After putting the colored pencils away, students can use what they've discovered to make a revision to-do list. By focusing on the more substantive items on their lists, they won't become fixated on word choice and spelling before their story structure is solid.

Often, I'll start making my to-do list while I'm writing my draft, and that keeps me from feeling stuck when I sit down to revise. I've been known to keep plowing through a rough draft, writing revision notes along the way: "In one hand, she held a length of thick rope and in the other, she clutched the WHAT DID I CALL THAT FUTURISTIC ZAPPING WEAPON? It was pointed straight at me." My students always laugh when I show them examples like this from my writing. It's comical, but let's face it, anything that can make us laugh along the rough road of revision is very welcome indeed.

After I finish drafting, I try to read through my manuscript, making big-picture notes. I ask questions in the margins and add notes all over the place. Figure 6.5 shows what my *Marty McGuire* manuscript looked like during one of my revision read-throughs.

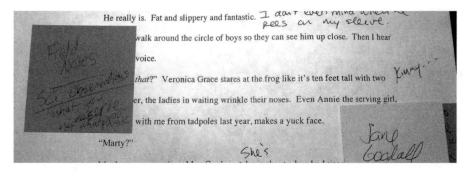

FIGURE 6.5

Marty McGuire, marked up during the revision process

Reading to Revise

When I'm reading to revise, I cross out words and phrases. I ask myself questions in the margin, and I make notes that will go on my to-do list. Some are specific: MENTION FROG HERE. Some will require a little more thought: MAKE THIS FUNNIER!

When I was working on a second draft of my middle-grades mystery, *The Star Spangled Setup*, my revision to-do list included the following:

- Tighten Chapter 3 (combine w/ 4?)
- Why is Henry so grumpy?
- Add Earl in earlier scene
- Need more suspicious behavior in Ch. 5
- Combine Ch. 6 and 7? Tighten both
- Mention snow in Ch. 6—storm needs to get worse
- Change lady from pub into man
- Anna needs to hear clinking sooner
- José—Why does he go around quoting people all the time?
- Ch. 19—Is it still snowing? Need to mention
- Ch. 22 needs more suspense—tighten
- Ch. 25—bring back rest of airport cast here—quick mentions

Creating a list like this makes an overwhelmingly big job feel more manageable. I might not know how to revise this whole novel, but by gosh, I can work on developing that one character so readers will know her better. When students can start their revision process with a manageable to-do list as well, they will feel more empowered. Who doesn't love crossing jobs off a list?

Tanya Lee Stone

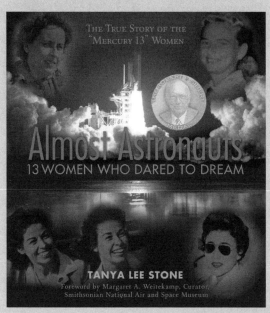

Tanya Lee Stone's nonfiction titles include *Elizabeth Leads the Way: Elizabeth Cady Stanton and the Right to Vote* (2008), which was both an ALA and a CBC Notable book and on the Amelia Bloomer List and Booklist's Top Ten, and *Almost Astronauts: 13 Women Who Dared to Dream* (2009)—a Boston Globe–Horn Book, NCTE Orbis Pictus, and Jane Addams Honor Book; YALSA Excellence in Nonfiction finalist; Bank Street's Flora Stieglitz Straus Award winner; and the Robert F. Sibert Medal winner. Her latest book is *The Good, the Bad, and the Barbie: A Doll's History and Her Impact on Us* (2010). Her Web site is www.tanyastone.com.

For each book, I ask myself the following questions: What is the most important part of the story, and what do the main characters (true characters in the case of nonfiction) need in order to fulfill what is important to them? Once I figure that out, I write a line or two that becomes my mantra for that book. Whenever I am stuck, or have a question about where I am going next, I refer to the mantra I've created.

TRY IT

What's the most important statement you can make about your piece of writing? Summarize the meaning in one sentence. Once you've found this theme, you will have what Tanya Lee Stone describes as the "mantra" for that piece of writing—the one sentence to which everything else on the page must return. The mantra can help guide your revision process. Here are some examples to inspire you:

Type of Writing	Possible Mantra
Persuasive letter about rain forest preservation	The world's rain forests are an important resource that must be preserved.
Poem about losing a pet	The feeling of missing follows you everywhere.
Personal narrative about winning a swim meet	Determination and lots of practice paid off in one exciting minute.
Short story about two friends who grow apart	People change as they grow, and sometimes old friends don't seem to fit any more.
Research paper about honey bees	Honey bees are an essential insect in nature.

Mantra Statement for My Work-in-Progress: _____

_____

_____

_____

_____

_____

Revision is like having
homework every night
for the rest of your life,
because your writing
never quite feels perfect.
But you have to embrace
the feeling and not mind
it, if you want to be a good
writer.

—SARAH ALBEE

CHAPTER 7

Returning to Research

S ometimes my revision to-do list sends me back to what we usually consider earlier stages in the writing process. We've talked about going back to brainstorming and back to planning, but what's a writer to do about notes on a manuscript like these?

FIND OUT WHAT A BEEHIVE SOUNDS LIKE.

WHAT'S UP WITH THE FUJITA SCALE?

HOW LONG DOES IT TAKE COMPOSTING WORMS TO EAT A PB&J CRUST?

All three are real scribbles from my manuscripts—scribbles that sent me back to the research stage as part of my revision.

Find Out What a Beehive Sounds Like

When I was revising *Sugar and Ice*, my editor Mary Kate asked me to work harder to show how the relationship between my main character, Claire, and her best friend, Natalie, changed when Claire started figure skating in Lake Placid. Wouldn't there be more tension? Maybe even an argument or blowup of some kind?

I found myself nodding as I read Mary Kate's notes. An argument between those two characters had been a long time coming, but I'd never actually written it into the book. Because I can't stand it when people just stand around talking in books, I wanted my characters to be doing something interesting while they argued. One of Natalie's hobbies was keeping bees; she tended the hives in her family's orchard, and I thought this would be a perfect place for the girls to have their showdown, with bees buzzing around them to add to the tension. So I added the scene. My writer friend Loree Griffin Burns wrote a book about honeybees, so I knew a thing or two about how hives were set up, and I described that in the scene, too.

But when I finished the passage and read it over, it still didn't ring true for me. I didn't *feel* like I was standing out at the hives with those two girls. I decided there weren't enough details to place readers at the scene, and I didn't have the right kind of experience to add them. So I called up Dave Greenwood, a local beekeeper, explained my problem, and asked if I might be able to visit him and his honeybees. (This is one of the greatest things about being an author. You can just call people up and ask them to show you stuff. They almost always say yes.) Dave was happy to have me visit his bees; in fact, he'd borrow an extra bee suit so I could work with him in the hives (see Figure 7.1).

My beekeeping date turned out to be on the hottest day of the summer. It was a sweaty afternoon, but a productive one. I brought my notebook and imagined what Claire would feel like, trying to talk to her friend while she dealt with the hives. I listened to the bees as Dave puffed smoke into their hives. They buzzed with a noise that sounded like sizzling bacon on an extra hot griddle. When they got upset, they flew at our veils as if they could buzz right through them. These are details I could not have made up; it was the research that allowed me to go back and revise the scene so that I was happy with it.

FIGURE 7.1
Ready for beekeeping research

What's Up with the Fujita Scale?

This note on the manuscript of my forthcoming dystopian novel, *Eye of the Storm* (2012), didn't require the same level of research—just a quick online search to find out more about the traditional scale used to measure a tornado's intensity—but it's another example of how revision sometimes involves research. Finding out about the current Enhanced Fujita scale enabled me to project what that scale might look like in a future where tornadoes had become more common and intense.

How Long Does It Take Composting Worms to Eat a PB&J Crust?

In *Marty McGuire Digs Worms* (2012), third-grade scientist Marty has to come up with a project to help the environment. While the other girls decide to grow flowers, Marty brings a worm farm into the cafeteria to eat the lunch scraps. When I was revising this manuscript, I had to think about the logistics. Would a newly established worm farm really be able to handle a whole lunchroom worth of kids' garbage? And what would happen to all the different stuff kids might try to feed them?

This time, research involved a trip to my local garden supply center to get myself set up for a little vermi-composting research. With help from my family, I assembled a worm bin in the basement and kept notes on how long it took the worms to eat different kinds of kitchen scraps. (See Figures 7.2 and 7.3.)

FIGURE 7.2

How long does it take the worms to turn kitchen scraps to compost?

FIGURE 7.3

Setting up the worm bin

Peanut-butter-and-jelly sandwich crusts, as it turned out, were not among the worms' favorite foods. Seeing the (extremely) slow process of that crust breaking down helped me to understand what poor Marty would be experiencing in her school lunchroom, wanting to show that her worms could tackle the school's garbage and being faced with the reality that they can't eat everything.

I love to share this example of research when I visit classrooms because so often students think of research as quiet, sitting-in-the-library time. Authors of books for young readers do plenty of quiet reading in libraries and online, to be sure, but they also conduct interviews and take some of the best field trips ever.

Jim Murphy says research helps him strengthen the voices of the people in his books about history. "After I wrote the opening chapter for *The Great Fire*, I wasn't happy with it, so I didn't work on the text for six months," he says. "During that time, I read newspaper and personal recollections of the Chicago fire until I had absorbed the pace and language of the era. Then I went back to the text, deleted what I'd done, and started over again. I didn't try to duplicate the voices from the past, but I knew I had a faint echo of them in my style."

Research is also a big part of the revision process for Kirby Larson, author of the Newbery Honor Book *Hattie Big Sky* (2006). When she's dealing with historical fiction, Larson says she strives to make sure she has an understanding of the time and place about which she's writing. Bibliographies of other books are great resources. "After that, it's always a balancing act between including those great details and turning the novel into a history textbook."

While Larson, Murphy, and I all write books for kids, our revising-with-research strategies would also work well as part of a unit on writing research papers. Often, we look at the process of writing a research paper as a linear one: brainstorm, research, plan, write, revise, edit, and publish. I'd argue that a better process would include a return to research during almost every step of the process.

One of my seventh-grade students, Addison, used this model beautifully as she worked on her Colonial America Diary entries. She'd spent several class periods doing research in the library, but when she began writing her diary entries, she quickly found that she wanted her colonial characters to do things that she had little research to support. A quick note to herself in the text ("how to make butter?") reminded her that a trip back to the library would be part of her revision process. She took another few pages of notes (see Figure 7.4).

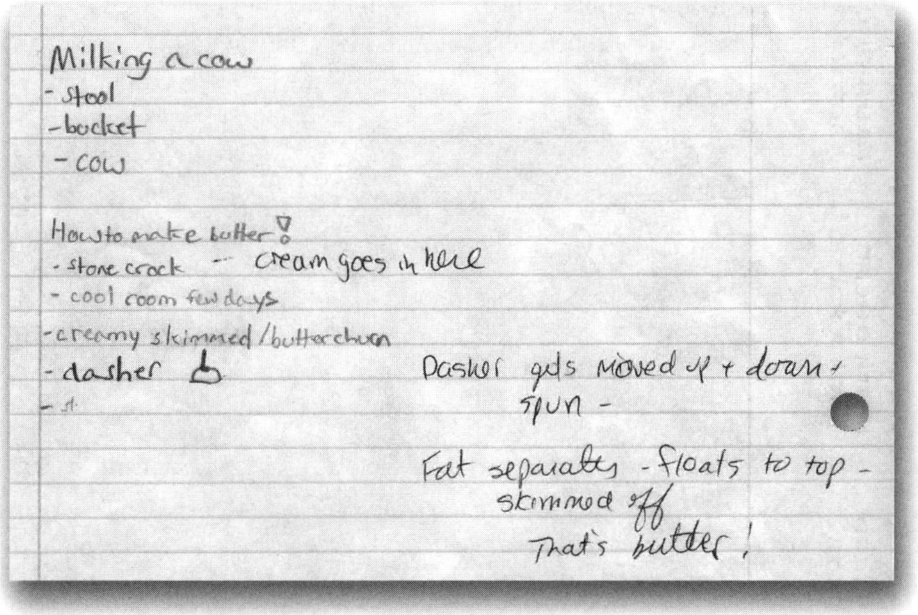

Milking a cow
- stool
- bucket
- cow

How to make butter?
- stone crock -- cream goes in here
- cool room few days
- creamy skimmed / butterchurn
- dasher

Dasher gets moved up + down + spun -

Fat separates - floats to top - skimmed off

That's butter!

FIGURE 7.4

Addison's "return-to-research" notes on milking a cow and making butter

As a result of that return to research, the final draft was rich with detail. Here's an excerpt from the diary entries Addison turned in:

> *June 9, 1750*
>
> *I have to get dressed quickly this morning so I can start my work day out in the fields that John and I own. As soon as I get outside into the fresh air, I start my work by going to the barn to milk my cow, Betty. I take two of Betty's udders and get to work. Pull, squeeze. Pull, squeeze. I start to see my pail fill up with fresh milk. Carrying my bucket off, I put some of the milk in a stone crock. I'll leave it there for a couple days, and then I will be able to take it out, skim off the creamy parts, and put them in my butter churn to start making some butter for Peter and Dorothy. Oh, how they love it on their bread during supper!*

Remember that revision activity where students marked up their persuasive essays with colored pencils? One of my students, Scott, noticed that due to his lack of blue pencil markings he had little evidence to support his argument that skateboarding should be offered as an activity in schools. He needed to return to the research process to find support for his thesis. (See Figure 7.5.)

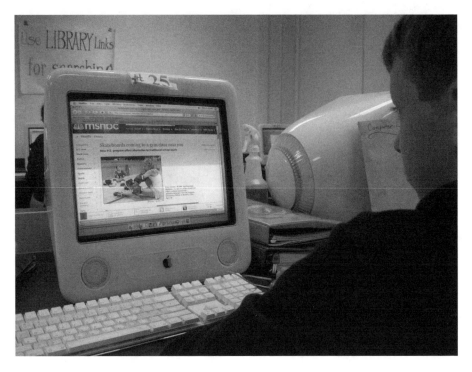

FIGURE 7.5
Scott gathers support for his persuasive argument.

Scott's revision-research process brought him to an online article from the Associated Press. It featured a Colorado school that offered skateboarding as part of its physical education curriculum. By showing that a model already existed for such a program, he was able to strengthen his argument.

Sometimes I've found that just knowing they have permission to return to an earlier step in the writing process helps kids move forward with a project. Revision, after all, means having a second chance to get it right.

Jim Murphy

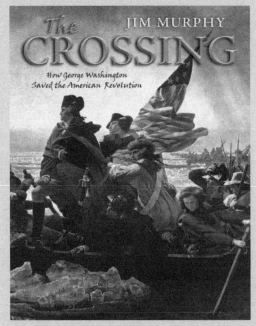

Jim Murphy has written more than thirty-five books for young readers, most of them dealing with American history and how children took an active part in shaping our country. His books have received many honors, including two ALA Newbery Honor Awards, an ALA Robert F. Sibert Medal, a Boston Globe–Horn Book Award for nonfiction, and three NCTE Orbis Pictus Awards. Jim recently received the ALA Margaret A. Edwards Award for his "significant and lasting contribution to young adult literature." His Web site can be found at www.jimmurphybooks.com.

I can usually find an image (drawing, painting, or photograph) of anyone mentioned in my texts. I study them carefully and write notes about the person and then work these details and observations into the text at appropriate places.

TRY IT

Find a picture—photograph, painting, drawing, sketch, or video—of the person about whom you're writing. That should be a simple library/Internet job if you're writing about a real person, but what if your characters are fictional? You can try using a photograph of someone you know or searching for a photo of a real person who might resemble your character. If your character is a girl with blond hair, for example, use whatever search tool your teacher recommends to search for images of "girl with blond hair" and see if one of those pictures looks like the image of the character in your head. Once you "find" your character, search for more details. Is that a birthmark on her chin? Does her hair always stick up on one side? Why is she tipping her head? And what is she looking at in the distance?

Take some time to study the image of your character and write down details. Later, look for good places to weave these details into your writing; you don't want to "dump" all the description in one spot!

Jane Yolen

Jane Yolen, called "the Hans Christian Andersen of America," is the author of more than 300 books, including *Owl Moon* (1987), *The Devil's Arithmetic* (1988), and *Dragon's Blood* (1982). Her books and stories have won an assortment of awards—two Nebula Awards, a World Fantasy Award, a Caldecott Medal, a Golden Kite Award, three Mythopoeic Fantasy Awards, two Christopher Medals, a Jewish Book Council Award, and a nomination for the National Book Award, among others. She is also the winner (for body of work) of the Kerlan Award, a Lifetime Achievement Award from the World Fantasy Organization, and the Regina Medal. Six colleges and universities have given her honorary doctorates. For more information, visit her Web site at www.janeyolen.com.

The lovely thing about writing is that you can put things in and take them out at any part of the process. So if I am revising and see that the characters are "floating," meaning there's nothing real anchoring them to the page, I can take time to go and do some more research—what birds would be singing in that place and that time of the year, or the kind of trees that are around, or particular dialects or a piece of clothing that is pertinent to the period, etc. As a poet, I know individual words are infinitely important, and I spend a lot of time making sure the right one is chosen.

TRY IT

Adding more setting details to a piece of writing can save your characters from "floating" and make your readers feel more deeply connected to a story. But sometimes adding those details means returning to research. Here's a quick research worksheet you can use to find more place-based details. Note: Imaginary places need details, too! If your world is a fantasy world or made-up planet, try basing it on a real country or planet. I know authors who base their fairy-tale castles on real castles in France or Germany and authors who have based their dystopian worlds on real-life locations that have experienced catastrophic events, such as Chernobyl.

My setting: _____

Research and take notes to provide details in the following categories:

Geography (mountains, rivers, deserts, oceans, etc.)

Weather (during the time of year when your piece of writing takes place)

Trees, flowers, and other plants that grow there

Insects that might be present (to "bug" your main character!)

Common animals

Birds

Popular foods of that place

Clothing

Other place-related notes for setting details

Revision is like weeding
because it's labor intensive
and difficult but once
you're done you're amazed
at the difference it made
. . . but you also know
that no matter how many
times you go through your
garden there will always
be more weeds to pull!

—ERIC LUPER

CHAPTER 8

Magic in the Details

When I visit schools to talk with students about writing, I often ask them what kinds of changes their teachers ask them to make when they're revising. The number one answer—it elicits nods and groans every time—is adding more details. Kids may be surprised to know that published authors get the same kinds of notes back from their editors, asking for more details and sensory language to make scenes and settings feel authentic.

Writers of science fiction and fantasy may have to imagine those concrete details, but they're not less important. Author Greg Fishbone (*The Penguins of Doom*, 2007) tries to include details that appeal to senses other than sight: "What does the inside of an alien spaceship smell like? What is the texture of the floors? What do the food dispensers sound like? These are questions I ask during the revision process because the first draft is more about what happens than exactly how it happens."

Students can use this model in the classroom after completing a draft. A separate read-through to focus on sensory details can be a huge help. Here, the colored pencils come in handy again. Give each student five different colored pencils, and assign each color a sense, like this:

Red = Sight
Blue = Hearing
Orange = Smell
Green = Touch
Purple = Taste

Ask students to read through their writing, underlining the specific details with the color that corresponds to the appropriate sense. A detail about chocolate chip cookies baking in the oven, for example, would be underlined in orange, because it appeals to the sense of smell, while a detail about the melted chocolate chips in someone's mouth would be underlined in purple. When students have finished this exercise, many may notice that their paper is very heavily slanted toward the color that corresponds to sight.

To help students expand on these sensory details, let them spend five to ten minutes focusing on each sense other than sight. For example, students might first pick up their blue colored pencils and read through their papers to find places where they might add details that relate to the sense of hearing. Encourage kids to ask themselves, "What would that sound like?" They can use their colored pencils to make notes in the margins about details they'd like to add in the next draft.

This is an activity that's easy to spread out over a few days when time in the schedule is tight. With just five minutes and one colored pencil each day, students can work with details that relate to all five senses during the week.

Sensory Field Trips

Sensory language is a great topic to tackle on a field trip day, even if that field trip is just down the hall. When I talk with my seventh-grade students about revising for word choice, I start by asking them to describe the school cafeteria while we sit in the classroom. They write quick paragraphs, and then I ask them to pack up their pencils and notebooks, and we go to the cafeteria. They spread out at tables and write. (See Figure 8.1.)

FIGURE 8.1

A seventh grader "collects" sensory words and phrases on a field trip to the cafeteria.

I give them directions to focus only on the sense of sight for the first few minutes. They note the shine of the floor, the faded red sweatshirt on the lost-and-found shelf, the big-screen television on the wall that was purchased to display announcements but never seems to be used. Then we switch senses.

"Turn off your eyes, and turn on your ears," I tell them. This time, they record only what they hear: the muffled clanging of pots and pans on the other side of the kitchen doors, the lunch ladies gossiping in the hallway, the slam of a locker door.

We continue with the senses of smell and touch, and when the students have finished, they have a list of sensory words and phrases to take back to the classroom. They use these terms to write a new descriptive paragraph, and they're amazed at how different, how much better, their new paragraphs are. (See Figures 8.2–8.4.)

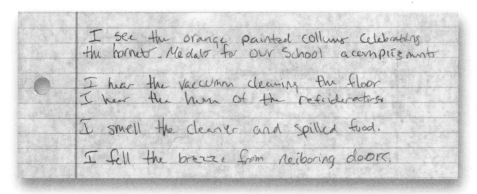

> I am sitting it the lunchroom after lunch. The room is quiet, like standing water, the only sounds comes from those of whom are still opening and shutting their lockers. The smell of spilled food and cleanser for the table swirl in the air.

FIGURE 8.2
First draft

> I see the orange painted collums celebrating the hornet. Medals for our school acomplizmnts
>
> I hear the vaccumm cleaning the floor
> I hear the hum of the refidieratrs
>
> I smell the cleaner and spilled food.
>
> I fell the brezze from neiboring doors.

FIGURE 8.3
Sensory detail notes

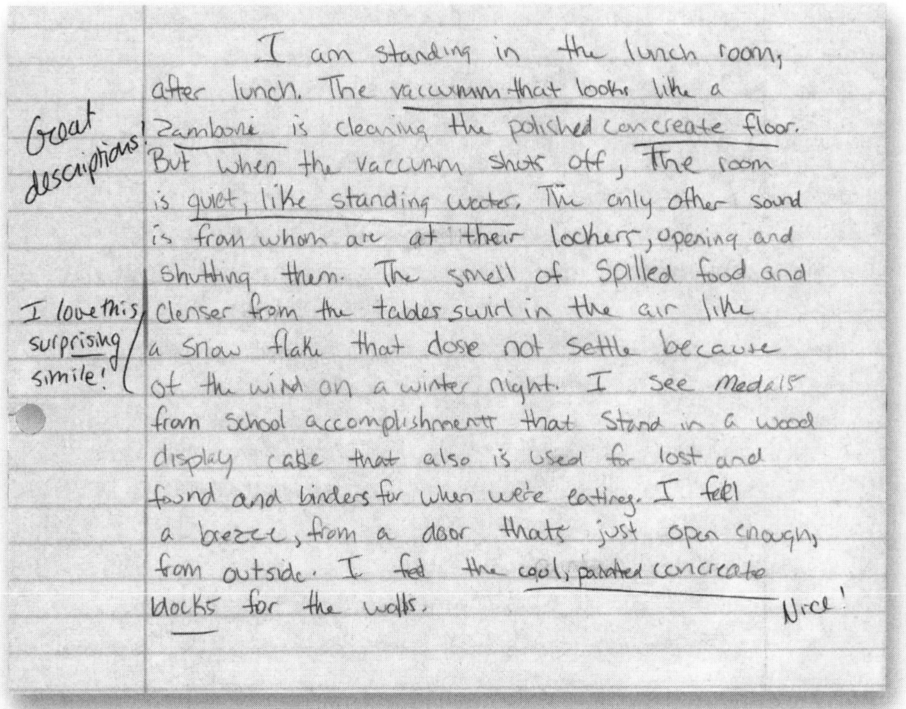

FIGURE 8.4
New draft

We take this activity a step further with a walking field trip outside on a warm September day. First, I share my poem "Sometimes on a Mountain in April" (2010), a multisensory celebration of spring in the mountains, written in free verse. I ask students to write a quick "Sometimes Outside in September" poem while sitting at their desks. Some struggle to come up with details, but they do their best.

After about ten minutes of writing, we put on sweatshirts and take a walk down the street to the monument across from our city hall. On a grassy slope that leads down to the riverbank, students repeat the activity we practiced in the cafeteria—isolating their senses to record the details they notice in descriptive language (see Figures 8.5 and 8.6). We bring digital cameras, too, to capture images to go along with the poems.

FIGURE 8.5

Mikayla brainstorms sensory details.

FIGURE 8.6

Nha-Thi uses her own "zoom lens" to look more closely at a fallen leaf.

We spend the next class period in the computer lab, weaving sensory details into our original poems, rewriting, and rethinking the idea of capturing a particular season in a particular moment. Figure 8.7 shows Hayden's first draft, compared to the later version after our sensory details walk shown in Figure 8.8.

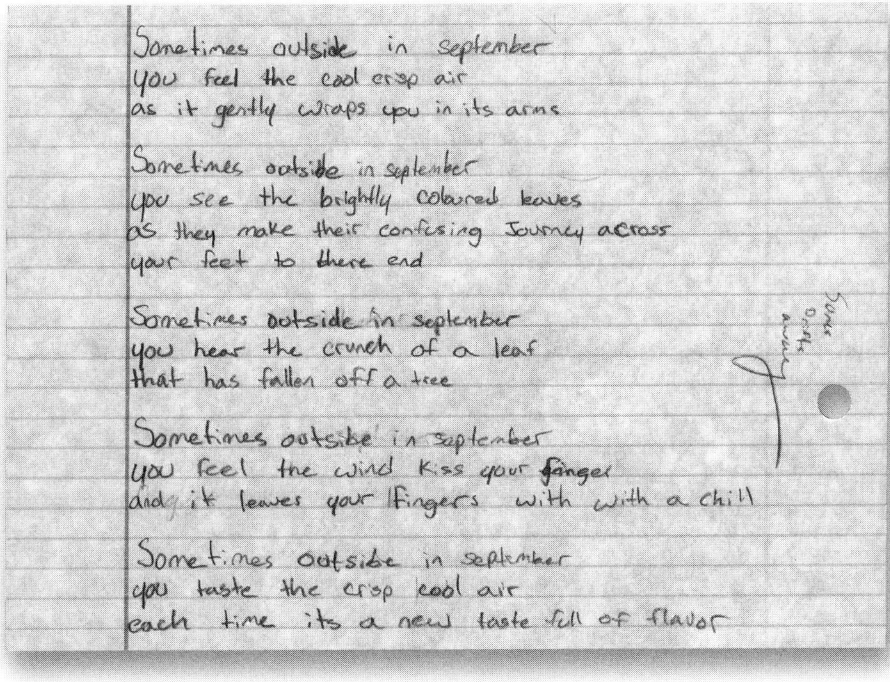

Sometimes outside in september
you feel the cool crisp air
as it gently wraps you in its arms

Sometimes outside in september
you see the brightly colored leaves
as they make their confusing journey across
your feet to there end

Sometimes outside in september
you hear the crunch of a leaf
that has fallen off a tree

Sometimes outside in september
you feel the wind kiss your finger
and it leaves your fingers with with a chill

Sometimes outside in september
you taste the crisp cool air
each time its a new taste full of flavor

FIGURE 8.7

Hayden's first draft

Hayden
8th period

Sometimes outside in September
The cool air gently wraps you in its arms
 And gives you a chill

Sometimes outside in September
Colored leaves blow past you
And drift away out of your reach

Sometimes outside in September
The sound of notes hitting the air and leaving forever
Sound like an autumn wind

Sometimes outside in September
If you look closely you see a village
Ants what wonderful critters they are
Lifting food and sliding over many types of grass
Long ones short ones big ones and little ones
They are all amazing we just never look close enough

Sometimes outside in September
You sit and enjoy the water rushing past
And you look taking in the sights
The fresh air with each breath brings a new scent
Warm lilies and fresh grass and soon they are gone
Never to be the same

Sometimes outside in September
You look at the marvelous river
Its water brown but only from the rocks that lay beneath
Splash what was that
A fish maybe a rock I may never know

Sometimes outside in September
You look and you see
A tree with bright green leaves
Not a single leaf missing
You wonder what kind of tree
Maple you say, could be
All that maters is that it's beautiful in every way

Sometimes outside in September
You look up you see warm fluffy clouds
A fish you see its body curved like it just exploded out of the water
Only to enter the water and turn into nothing other than a cotton ball

Sometimes outside in September
You close your eyes and think of winter what will it bring
Cold snow or just cold air you may not know
You open your eyes to see summer slowly slipping beyond your reach.

FIGURE 8.8

Hayden's final draft

Field Trip (and Virtual Field Trip!) Research

When writing about a real place, it can be helpful to take a field trip with a notebook to gather those little details that are impossible to imagine. To revise *Sugar and Ice*, which is set in part on a maple farm, I purposely waited until sugaring season to focus on the details.

I grew up in New York State, and I'd been to pancake breakfasts before, but visiting a maple farm with my camera and notebook in hand (see Figure 8.9) enabled me to look more closely; to notice that late-March mix of snow, mud, and slush on the ground; and to remember that some people eat dill pickles with their pancakes and syrup, a detail too weird to make up. When I turned in my final draft, those scenes set on the farm were some of my editor's favorites, and I know that being there, breathing in the maple steam, was part of what made them resonate.

FIGURE 8.9
Parker Family Maple Farm, where I took photographs, scribbled notes, and ate too many pancakes while writing *Sugar and Ice*

Cynthia Lord, the author of *Touch Blue* (2010) and the Newbery Honor Book *Rules* (2006), also likes to visit her books' settings whenever she can. Cindy attended a writing retreat that I organized for children's book authors on Lake Champlain, and one afternoon, we noticed she was missing from the inn. She'd spent several hours sitting by the shore, gathering information for her new book, which is set on a lake in New Hampshire.

"I was taking down sensory details," she said, "because I find that I can write things like conversations and scenes at home, but if I'm going to write setting, I really like to be there because there are all those little things that you don't even recognize when you're writing unless you see them and you hear them. When I just imagine, I'm often imagining things I've seen on TV or read in someone else's book, but when I'm actually in a setting I will hear those little surprising details and those are the things that bring a description to life."

What kinds of details made it into her notebook that afternoon? "Just hearing the train go by . . . I wouldn't think about a train when you're at a lakeside but it felt very real that trains go near lakes. So I wrote that down. I wrote down what colors the rocks were, and they were colors that sometimes surprised me a little bit. I wrote down that it's sort of a fizzle and a hiss when a wave comes up and ends and then when it starts back there's that sort of bubbling sound. And I sat there a long time listening to it and trying to put that into words that would call up for the reader what I heard, so it's all those little details. Like bugs—I never imagined bugs, but as I walked around, I saw this beautiful blue dragonfly."

Writers of nonfiction rely on site visits and interview notes to add details during the revision process as well. "I generally go back to my research to remind myself of all the sensory details I discovered at the time," says Tanya Lee Stone, the author of *Almost Astronauts* (2009) and many other works of nonfiction for kids. "For example, if I interviewed someone, I will note very specific things about the way they speak, move, dress, smell, etc. These details come in handy when writing a scene that needs to capture the real essence of a person."

But what about when our students don't have access to the people and places about which they're writing? How can we achieve that same sense of wonder in the classroom?

Try leaving it once in a while.

If only for ten minutes, let students grab notebooks and pencils, and take them on a detail-gathering field trip to the pond near the school, or the playground, or the gym. Ask them to use all of their senses and really pay attention to the unexpected details. Getting kids used to this level of observation can help them bring more imagery to their writing, even when an actual site visit isn't possible.

Drawing memory maps can help students revise when they're writing personal narratives set in a place they've lived or visited. My seventh-grade student Risha found that drawing the land around her grandfather's home in India helped her to recall the vivid details that were part of her visit over the summer (see Figure 8.10).

FIGURE 8.10

Risha's map of her grandfather's property in India

AN EXCERPT FROM RISHA'S PERSONAL NARRATIVE

I wake up at 6 am hearing the sound of the mill timekeeper down the road banging the gong to

wake up all of the workers. I can smell wet dew and my grandmother's potato cakes on the stove.

My thin blanket from last night has rolled down to the floor. I go outside to get a good stretch.

As soon as I reach the porch I see a camel with a decorative saddle on his back and a herd of

cows that in India we call the "guys." A man has a stick in his hand and is hitting the cows if they

don't move in the right direction.

What happens when our students are writing about a place they've never had an opportunity to visit? Technology can aid the revision process with a virtual field trip. Author G. Neri uses online maps and satellite images to help make sure his settings are authentic. "For *Ghetto Cowboy*, I even gave the illustrator Google Earth points at street level, where he could see actual buildings and sometimes even the people in the neighborhoods."

Google Earth is a great revision tool for kids, too, especially when brainstorming details. Students can write about a city on the other side of the world and gather details by checking out those street-level images. What kinds of stores are on a street? What color is the dirt? What are the people wearing? And from there, students can begin to imagine other sensory details. What might that cornfield sound like in the wind? How might that Dumpster smell on a hot day?

Write Here, Right Now

As I finish this chapter, I'm sitting in my writing room at home, looking out the window. Can you envision it?

No?

Let me try again.

Outside the window over my desk, a south wind is whipping up whitecaps on Lake Champlain. They're whooshing and shushing on the rocks. The island a mile offshore is the hazy dark green of late summer, and soon the treetops will be blending into the golds and reds of September. We were away last week, so the deck chairs are naked skeletons around the table, their floral cushions tucked away in the shed. The tomatoes droop, overripe in the garden, and the lawn needs a haircut.

How about now?

Students can do the same kind of writing and rewriting in the classroom, working with a friend. Write a little. Add details. Can you see it yet? Can you hear it? Smell it?

How about now?

Sensory details are the magic ingredients that transport readers into a piece of writing.

Loree Griffin Burns

Loree Griffin Burns's first career was as a research scientist (she holds a PhD in biochemistry), and her writing celebrates the natural world and the people who study it. Her first book for young people, *Tracking Trash: Flotsam, Jetsam, and the Science of Ocean Motion* (2007), received starred reviews in *Kirkus* and *School Library Journal* as well as several honors, including an International Reading Association Children's Book Award and being named both a Boston Globe–Horn Book Honor Book and an ALA Notable Book. Her second book, *The Hive Detectives*, was released in 2010 and is creating a little buzz of its own! Learn more at her Web site: www.loreegriffinburns.com.

Because I write nonfiction and am often describing actual scenes, I take careful notes in the field. These notes encompass all my sensorial experiences . . . the sounds, the smells, the sights, the textures I see and feel, and sometimes even the way things taste. I may need these details later, and I have made recording them a habit. I often close my eyes so that I can concentrate on my other senses, then snap them open and jot down what I heard, felt, and smelled.

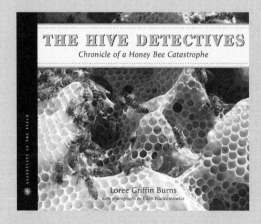

TRY IT

Great descriptive writing appeals to more than just one or two senses. You can train yourself to include sensory details by practicing paying attention to your surroundings and by focusing on one sense at a time. Choose a setting—something as simple as your classroom or the sidewalk outside is just fine—and spend one minute writing only details about what you see. When you finish, turn your eyes "off" and turn your ears "on," and focus only on what you hear. Spend a minute or two writing details that you notice relating to each of the four senses. (Use that fifth sense of taste only if there's actually food present!)

What do you see?	What do you hear?	What do you feel?	What do you smell?	What do you taste?

Sara Lewis Holmes

Sara Lewis Holmes began her first novel, *Letters from Rapunzel,* by imagining that her main character was writing letters from captivity. The novel won the Ursula Nordstrom Fiction Prize and was published in 2007. She followed it with a story drawn straight from the life of her military family, *Operation Yes* (2009). Sara has lived in eleven states and three countries. She now lives in Virginia with her husband and two children. Her Web site is www.saralewisholmes.com.

In Operation Yes there's a scene between Bo and his new theater-loving teacher, Miss Loupe, in which she insists he learn to fall down safely before she'll teach him any stage combat moves. My editor said she wasn't feeling the scene as written on the page, so I went to my yoga teacher for help. My yoga teacher also happens to be trained in theater and dance, so

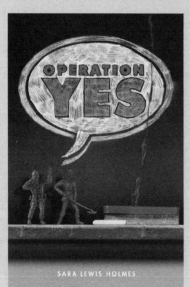

with her guidance, I literally fell down, over and over (on a nice soft carpet), to experience what a stage fall feels like from the inside. Later, I was able to translate that body knowledge to the page.

And even later, when I had the fun of going to Shakespeare Camp one summer, I was thrilled to learn choreography for a sword fight, and guess what the ending of the duel was? Why, a stage fall! I collapsed, carefully and realistically, to the floor.

TRY IT

Acting out a scene in your story can be a great way to find more vivid details to include from your character's point of view. Find a scene in your story that might work, and enlist the help of a friend if needed. With a notebook nearby, act out your character's movements. Is he or she falling? Sneaking into a room? What do you notice about how your body moves when you act out the sequence? How does it feel? Jot down those details in your notebook, and then you'll be ready to go back and add them to the scene when you revise.

Cynthia Lord

Cynthia Lord's debut novel, *Rules* (2006), was a 2007 Newbery Honor Book and Schneider Family Book Award winner. She also wrote *Touch Blue* (2010) and *Hot Rod Hamster* (2010), a picture book for younger readers. Cynthia Lord grew up in New Hampshire and taught school before she began writing for children. She now lives in Maine with her family, and you can visit her at her Web site: www.cynthialord.com.

I was writing the scene in **Rules** *where Catherine and Jason [who is in a wheelchair] go running in the parking lot. He admits to her that sometimes when he's asleep, he dreams that he can run, and he asks her, "What does that feel like?" And she tries to put that into words, but it's actually really hard to tell somebody what it feels like to run. . . . She just feels so bad for him that she makes that joke that they can go out in the parking lot and she'll push him and that will feel like running. He says okay. So then she has to do it.*

When I was going to write that, I thought I needed to sort of experience that because when you're walking, you're looking at a very different view than when you're pushing somebody. When you're pushing somebody, you're paying so much attention to everything that's down on the ground, everything you have to make decisions about, whether you'll go around it or over it. . . .

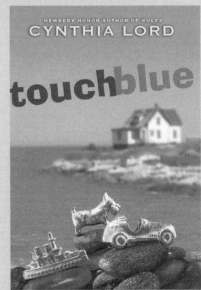

So I didn't have a wheelchair, and I started to think of what sorts of things have wheels that I could push around a parking lot and have that experience . . . so I brought a rolling suitcase. I pulled up the handle and I walked all around the parking lot, rolling my suitcase over the sewer grate, the pinecones, the sticks, and those were the kinds of things I had to make those choices about, like Catherine did. . . . All those little details ended up in the book, because that's what made it feel more real to people.

TRY IT

When it's not possible to act out a scene from your story, you might be able to find a "substitute activity" like Cynthia Lord's rolling-suitcase walk. Read through your piece of writing. What scene includes an experience you've never had and can't create easily or safely? You may still be able to gather details for that scene with an experience that puts you in your character's shoes.

If your character is being chased, for example, try running as fast as you can, imagining someone behind you. What happens to your body? Your heart rate? What if your character has injured his or her arm by falling into a pit? (I hope this has never happened to you!) Try binding one arm to your side with a scarf and climbing with just your legs and other arm to get a sense of how difficult fast-paced movement might be with those restrictions.

Brainstorm a list of situations in your story with possible substitute activities that might help you to add details!

Situation _____

Possible substitute activity_____

Situation_____

Possible substitute activity _____

Situation_____

Possible substitute activity_____

Revision is like getting
everyone in the choir to
sing in harmony because
if one voice sticks out, it
ruins it for everyone else.

—KATHI APPELT

CHAPTER 9

Are the People Real?

s an author, I know my characters are real when I start shopping for them. More than once, while browsing in a store, I have spotted the perfect scarf or art-themed pin. "Oh my gosh!" I thought, rushing over to pick it up. "Gianna would love this!"

I put the pin back on the shelf when my husband gently reminded me that most people don't actually make purchases for their imaginary friends.

But I'm always thankful for those moments because it means a character in my work-in-progress has crossed a line from a person on the page to a real person in my mind, and, I hope, in my readers' minds, too.

As writers, how do we make such transformations happen? Usually it takes time, just as it takes time to get to know a new friend in real life. You need to get over that awkward, first-meeting nervousness when all you really talk about are superficial topics like the weather. Investing more time and interest, you go deeper and figure out what that person likes to do on a Saturday afternoon. As an author you must learn the character's deepest, darkest secrets—what she wants more than anything in the world or what he fears the most. For many authors, this deeper level of knowing characters doesn't occur until well after the first draft has been completed, so character development becomes a major part of the revision process.

Becoming Our Characters

I'm writing this chapter about characters and revision on a plane, coming home from a research trip to Oklahoma. I spent yesterday at the University of Oklahoma and the National Weather Center, where the National Severe Storms Laboratory is located. This was a research trip for my forthcoming dystopian novel, *Eye of the Storm*.

In one giant room filled with computers and radar screens, I watched meteorologists following the path of Hurricane Earl as it headed for the East Coast. I spent time with Dr. Howard Bluestein, a well-known meteorologist and storm chaser. All the while, I wished that Jaden, my main character in *Eye of the Storm*, could have been there with me. She would have loved it. She'd be fighting me for this window seat right now, too, because the clouds over the Midwest are spectacular. Although this research trip was more about the science behind this novel than the characters, I feel like imagining Jaden in this new context helped me to know her better than I did before I came.

Aside from spending time thinking about characters, writers can explore the people who inhabit their stories in a variety of ways. We can interview characters, map out sketches of their bedrooms, journal in their voices, question their friends and their enemies, and—piece by piece—build lives for them.

When I was writing *Sugar and Ice*, one of the things my editor asked for during the revision process was a better window into my main character Claire's life at school. I sat down at my computer but typed for only a minute or two before I realized that I needed to take a step back. What did Claire's day at school even look like? Because she's a seventh grader when the book begins, I modeled her schedule loosely after the one my own seventh-grade students follow. I played the role of Claire's guidance counselor and made a course schedule for her, to show not only when she had classes like math and science, but also which courses she shared with her best friend, Natalie, and when the two of them might have time to chat at school (see Figure 9.1). This helped me add the school scenes that my editor requested in a way that felt believable and consistent.

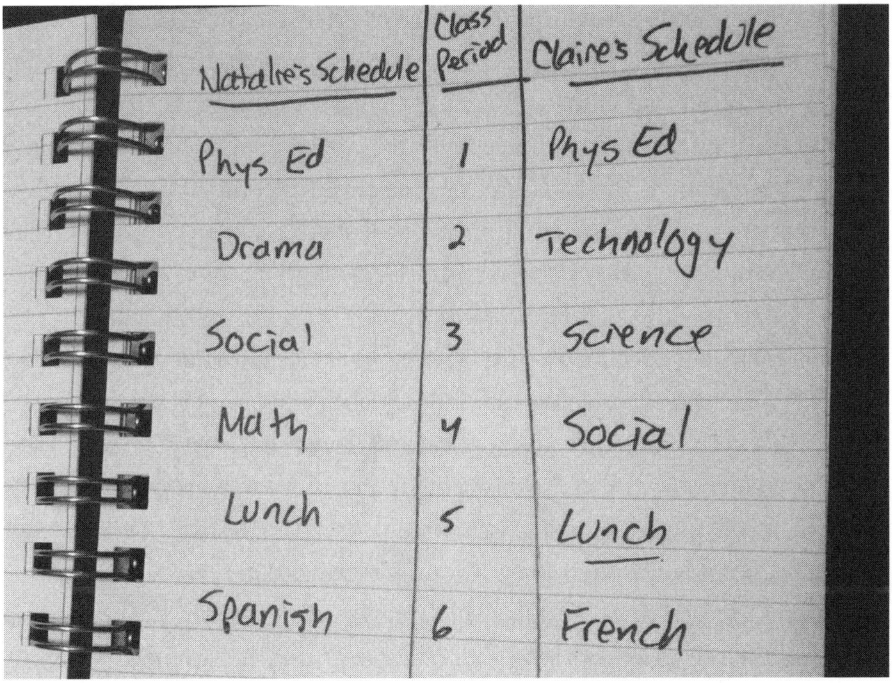

FIGURE 9.1

School-day schedules for Claire and Natalie

As I dug deeper and deeper into this story, I found myself asking over and over, "What does Claire really want?" Getting at the heart of a person almost always means answering that question.

Kathryn Erskine, author of *Mockingbird* (2010), recommends interviewing the characters in a story. "Sit down somewhere comfortable with your laptop or a pad of paper and ask them what they like and don't like, where they'd like to travel, their favorite things to do, and question number one: 'What do you want?' That'll get at the character's motivation, what's really important, and, subconsciously, it's getting at why this story is important to you."

Lisa Schroeder, author of *It's Raining Cupcakes* (2010), uses a similar method. "I like to ask my characters questions," she says, "like what posters do you have on your wall, what music do you listen to, and who would you call first if you got really good news." Schroeder also freewrites about earlier times in her characters' lives "to figure out why they are the way they are."

Students in my seventh-grade creative writing elective use character questionnaires and interviews (see the Try It in Lisa Schroeder's Mentor Author section on page 125 and in the appendix) to help them develop their characters more fully during the revision process. It's important not only to provide a list of guideline questions for students to use as a starting point, but also to leave this activity open-ended enough to allow students to go off on tangents as they explore characters, perhaps stopping to freewrite or develop one particular aspect of the individual's personality more fully.

Joni Sensel, author of *The Farwalker's Quest* (2009), seeks to know a character's history. "I sometimes do time lines for individual characters," she says, "to figure out how old they would have been at various points in a story, or when they must have been born." She also asks characters about their secrets. "What's under their bed? Under the underwear and socks in that drawer? What would they never admit to anyone? That's always inspiring to me."

Karen Day, author of *A Million Miles from Boston* (2011), brainstorms in a journal, trying to discover things her characters may not even know about themselves. "I have to know what every character wants on an unconscious level as well, which gets really complicated," she says. But it helps her to have well-rounded characters. "For example, in *A Million Miles from Boston*, I knew that I wanted Ian to tease my main character, Lucy, and that this teasing would have a mean streak. When Ian eventually shows up in Maine, at Lucy's summer cottage, we cringe because we know their history. But why does he tease her? Then I figured out that he does this because Lucy reminds him of his sister, who is nasty to him, only he's not conscious of this. Neither is Lucy. But because I have this knowledge (as the author) I can make this more focused. *You think you know everything!* He yells at Lucy. But really he's talking to his sister."

Jody Feldman, author of *The Gollywhopper Games* (2008), tries to come up with little details that distinguish characters from one another. "Like the way she bites her lips. Or his keeping an emergency 3 Musketeers bar. Or her hair that always slips out of the ponytail. Or the fact he drops things when he's nervous. It's the little details that make each blond-haired, blue-eyed, twelve-year-old suburban school girl different from the eight other near-clones standing with her in the school cafeteria."

Often, those little details are the hardest thing to imagine, so it helps to base characters on real people. Nora Raleigh Baskin, the author of *Anything but Typical* (2009), says she always has some real person in mind, "even if it's the tour guide I heard at the museum or the check-out girl in the grocery store."

Collecting Character Details

Sometimes, when I have waiting time in the grocery store or at an airport, I'll do some "character research" in my notebook. I look around and collect details about my fellow travelers or shoppers.

It's the tiny details—the tall white socks with the hiking boots and the oversized sunglasses—that would be almost impossible for me to imagine, yet those details are often the most vivid. I can't remember which book I was working on when I "collected" this man in my notebook (see Figure 9.2), but bits of his description may come in handy in a future novel.

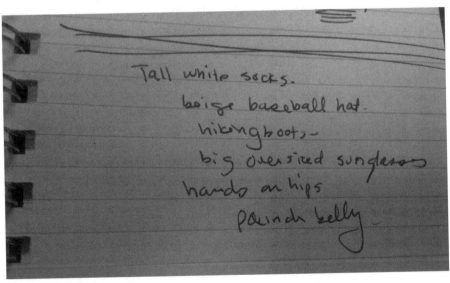

FIGURE 9.2
A character-research page from my notebook

Students can take part in a similar character-detail collection activity right at school. Without naming names, they can jot down details about their class-mates—the way one boy twirls his shoelaces or the way the girl by the window taps her pencil against her cheek while she works on math problems—for use in future writing projects.

Mitali Perkins, author of *Bamboo People* (2010), says it's also important to think about how a character moves. "I try to consider the non-verbals of each character in each scene. How would they be standing? What are their facial expressions? How far apart from each other? What are they holding?"

Sometimes, character development comes easily for a main character, but other characters might be reluctant to come to life on the page. Author Erin Dionne says she always ends up developing minor characters more fully during the revision process. "Their personalities don't come out real well at first," Dionne says. Her editor gave her a great strategy for working with secondary characters. "She said that in every scene where a minor character appears, we should learn something new about them. It doesn't have to be anything major. It might just be the color of their sneakers or something else, so you get to know them and they become more complex as the story goes on."

For example, in her upcoming novel *Notes from an Accidental Band Geek* (2011), Dionne found herself returning to a secondary character named Hector. "He's obsessed with *Star Wars*, so I started giving him funny T-shirts and *Star Wars* accessories in every scene."

Villains pose another problem. "I always have one or two characters that feel flat to me, and I have no idea how to fix them. Mainly bad guys," says Watt Key, author of *Alabama Moon* (2006) and *Dirt Road Home* (2010). "I just don't know any real bad people, so when I write about them, I always feel like I'm making it all up—which I am—and sometimes that comes through and makes them flat."

Katie Davis, author of *The Curse of Addy McMahon* (2008), had trouble exploring the personality traits of one of her villains. "I gave myself a writing exercise where I told the story from her point of view—this was after I was very close to my heroine and really hated this nemesis character," Davis says. "I gave her a hobby, likes and dislikes, fave foods and colors, and a secret. It allowed me to see her as a more fully rounded person rather than some character on a piece of paper."

In my figure-skating novel, *Sugar and Ice*, the main character encounters some other skaters with pretty sharp edges when she goes to train in Lake Placid.

I had to develop life histories for each of these girls. How long had they been skating? What were their families like? How much pressure was there at home? Most of those details never made it into the final book, but as an author, it was important for me to understand what made these characters tick—what could drive someone to cross over from competitive to downright mean?

Speaking Parts

Of course, what a character says (and chooses not to say!) speaks volumes about the character's psyche. Part of my revision process for dialogue involves reading each character's dialogue aloud—just the words in quotes from that one character—to make sure his or her particular voice rings true consistently. If one of my characters suddenly sounds a lot like another one, I know it's time to rewrite some of that dialogue.

Author Danette Haworth's first two books, *Violet Raines Almost Got Struck by Lightning* (2008) and *The Summer of Moonlight Secrets* (2010), are set in the South, and she made an effort to let her characters' language reflect their upbringing and personalities. "A tip I picked up along the way was to take familiar patterns of speech and make them peculiar to your character," Haworth says. "Violet Raines lives in a rural, old-Florida small town. There is a scene in which Violet is extremely sure things are going to happen in a certain way, but instead of having her say, 'I'll eat my hat if . . .' I had Violet say, 'I'll eat gator tail if . . .' It fit her character and her independent spirit!"

Name Games

In addition to tweaking dialogue, many authors change characters' names during the revision process, trying to come up with the perfect moniker for each person in the book. Sometimes, the names come from characters in books or history. Sometimes, they're chosen to honor friends. And sometimes, a name just sounds right for a particular character.

In *The Brilliant Fall of Gianna Z.*, for example, the name Gianna came from a music teacher at the school where I teach; I just liked the way it sounded and thought it was a good name for someone with a creative spirit. The name Zig came to me out of the blue, and since it's an unusual name, I needed it to be short for something else, so I came up with the full name Kirby Zigonski. Gianna's friend Ruby, whose family doesn't have much money, was named for Ruby Payne, the author of a book for educators about understanding poverty. Bianca just felt like a good "mean girl" name to me (I am sorry if you are named Bianca . . . I'm sure you are very nice!). Gianna's Coach Napper was named for a science teacher at my school who assigned kids the leaf project that inspired this book.

In *Sugar and Ice*, the main character is Claire because that's a name I liked and it fit with her family's French Canadian ancestry. Many of the other skaters—Alexis, Meghan, and Kianna—were named for young figure skaters in my community who helped me by answering technical questions about the jumps and spins as I was writing and revising. Other secondary characters such as Hannah, Rory, and Natalie were named after some of my students. I searched Russian names online to come up with Claire's Lake Placid coach, Andrei Groshev. And her coach at the home rink, Mary Kate, was named for my editor at Walker/Bloomsbury, Mary Kate Castellani. Editors, after all, are a whole lot like coaches in the way they help us perfect our work, so it seemed like a fitting match!

Where do other authors find inspiration for character names? Here's a sampling of ideas:

Names come from people I've known or people I've heard about. Dogie's name, in *Keeper*, came from an old western TV show I used to watch when I was little. I confess that I love naming my characters—just like I love naming cats.
—**KATHI APPELT, AUTHOR OF** *THE UNDERNEATH* **AND** *KEEPER*

Sometimes I borrow names from people I know. In *Neil Armstrong Is My Uncle* I used the names of friends and my sister. The main character's best friend is named Kebsie. I made up that name with my two best friends from high school. We combined our names. The *K* is from Kate, the *eb* is from Deb, and the *sie* sound comes from my name, Nancy.

—NAN MARINO, AUTHOR OF *NEIL ARMSTRONG IS MY UNCLE*

I collect names by reading obituaries and baby name books and scouring the Social Security Web site that lists the top 100 names of each decade. Names are crucial! Once I had a picture book that just wasn't working until I changed the main character's name from Katerina to Griselda—the perfect name for a grumpy old lady.

—KIRBY LARSON, AUTHOR OF *HATTIE BIG SKY*

Wendy Mass

Wendy Mass is the author of ten novels for young people (which have been translated into twelve languages and nominated for forty state book awards). Her books include *Jeremy Fink and the Meaning of Life* (2006), *11 Birthdays* (2009), *Every Soul a Star* (2008), *The Candymakers* (2010), and *A Mango-Shaped Space* (2005), which was awarded the Schneider Family Book Award by the American Library Association. She wrote the story line for an episode of the television show *Monk*, entitled "Mr. Monk Goes to the Theatre," which aired during the show's second season. Wendy tells people her hobbies are hiking and photography, but really she prefers collecting candy-bar wrappers and searching for buried treasure with her metal detector. She lives with her family in New Jersey. Visit her at http://wendymass.com.

If I can't picture characters and hear them, then I know I have to go back and give them more personality traits or habits or quirks. I have a biography sheet for each main character that I fill out very thoroughly before I start writing, so that helps to make them feel real even before I really get to know them.

Wendy Mass shares her character sheet for David, a character in a new novel she's working on, set in the same world as *11 Birthdays*.

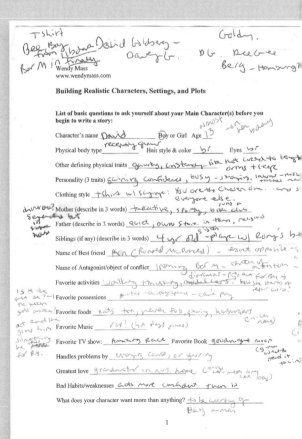

TRY IT

Try out the biography sheet that Wendy Mass uses for her novels. Answer as many questions as you can about the main person in your piece of writing.

Character Biography

Character's name_____

Boy or Girl_____   Age_____

Physical description _____

Hair style & color_____   Eyes _____

Other defining physical traits_____

Personality (3 traits) _____

Clothing style_____

Mother (describe in 3 words)_____

Father (describe in 3 words) _____

Siblings (if any) (describe in 3 words) _____

Name of best friend_____

Name of antagonist/enemy/object of conflict_____

Favorite activities_____

Favorite things he/she owns _____

Favorite foods _____

Favorite music_____

Favorite TV show _____

Favorite book _____

Handles problems by_____

Greatest love _____

Bad habits/weaknesses _____

What does your character want more than anything? _____

_____

_____

_____

_____

_____

G. Neri

G. Neri is the ALA Notable author of *Chess Rumble* (2007) and the winner of the 2010 IRA Lee Bennett Hopkins Promising Poet Award. His other books for middle graders include his new graphic novel *Yummy: The Last Days of a Southside Shorty* (2010), and the upcoming novel *Ghetto Cowboy* (2011). He currently lives on the Gulf Coast of Florida with his wife and daughter. Visit his Web site: www.gregneri.com.

Years ago, I started collecting names from spam e-mails that were computer generated. I ended up with an incredibly rich list of names and that's the first place I go when I start writing. Those names have character.

TRY IT

Start your own collection of character names. They don't have to come from unwanted e-mail addresses like G. Neri's; names are everywhere. Jot down names of kids in your class that you like. Who has a last name that would make a good first name? The phone book has many names to choose from. Try skimming through the pages, and keep a list of your favorites.

First Names for Girls	First Names for Boys	Last Names

Lisa Schroeder

Lisa Schroeder is the author of four novels for young adults, including the popular *I Heart You, You Haunt Me* (2008). *It's Raining Cupcakes* (2010) is her first middle-grades novel. She lives in Oregon with her husband and two sons. Her Web site is www.lisaschroederbooks.com.

I read one time that every character, not just the main character, should want something. The trick, then, is to find out WHY each character wants what they want. That can tell you a lot about a character. Sometimes we have to spend time thinking and freewriting about earlier times in the character's life to figure out why they are the way they are. I like to ask my characters questions, too, like what posters do you have on your wall, what music do you listen to, and who would you call first if you got really good news?

TRY IT

Go beyond the original biography sheet you filled out for your character and interview him or her. You can do this in writing if you want, or you can even set up a microphone and video camera to record both "sides" of the interview. Here's a list of questions to get you started!

What does your bedroom look like?

What's under your bed?

Who has disappointed you?

What is your secret dream?

What do you want/need right now?

What are some of your favorite songs and why?

If you got really good news, who would you call first?

What do you like most about yourself?

What would your parents say is your greatest flaw?

What would your friends say is your greatest flaw?

What do you believe in?

Eric Luper

Eric Luper is the author of several YA books, including *Seth Baumgartner's Love Manifesto* (2010). His first middle-grades novel is *Jeremy Bender Vs. the Cupcake Cadets* (2011). Originally from New Jersey, Eric currently calls Albany, New York, home, where he writes, spends time with his family, and tries to get to Lake George as often as possible. His Web site is www.ericluper.com.

I make sure I know more about my characters than I'll ever convey in the story. Likes/dislikes, strengths/weaknesses, habits/hobbies, etc. If a character feels flat, I didn't do a good enough job developing him or her. Names usually come to me early on and help guide who the character is. Sometimes it's the other way around. When I am character building, often I create a hybrid of people I know. Then, as the character develops through the story I fine-tune who they are.

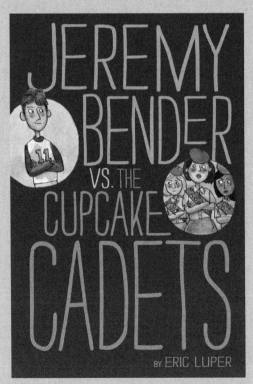

TRY IT

Some of Eric Luper's characters are a hybrid, or mix, of people he knows. Blending qualities of actual people you know is a great strategy for coming up with characters who have realistic traits and personalities. To begin, list three people you know in the column on the left. Then fill in the information about those three people (only positive, kind observations, please!). When you've finished, you can use the list to blend the traits and qualities and create a new hybrid character.

Person's name/ initials	Physical description (hair color, eye color, etc.)	Something the person loves/is good at	Something the person doesn't like	Unusual quirk or detail about this person	Other notes

Tom Angleberger

Tom Angleberger is a newspaper reporter/columnist, semiprofessional juggler, amateur square-dance caller, and the author of *The Strange Case of Origami Yoda* (2010) and *Stonewall Hinkleman and the Battle of Bull Run* (2009). His latest book is *Horton Halfpott* (2011). Tom's Web site is http://origamiyoda.wordpress.com.

The drawings I did for Origami Yoda *and* Horton Halfpott *really helped make the characters real and clear. In both cases, these drawings were done before many of the revisions. I'm thinking of trying the same thing on my next book—creating portraits as part of the writing process.*

TRY IT

Write a quick paragraph about your main character's appearance. Now take a few minutes and draw that character, including as much detail as you can. It's okay if you're not an artist! But try to notice the little things about this character—decide which way his or her hair is parted and whether or not it sticks up around the ears. After you've had a chance to finish your drawing, go back and revise your character paragraph to add more details.

Donna Gephart

Donna Gephart's latest novel, *How to Survive Middle School* (2010), received starred reviews from *Kirkus* and *School Library Journal*. Her first book, *As if Being 12¾ Isn't Bad Enough, My Mother Is Running for President* (2008), won the Sid Fleischman Humor Award. Donna lives in South Florida with her family. Visit her at www.donnagephart.com.

Dealing with an Ex-Best Friend, a New *Girl* Best Friend and a Heart-Breaking Hamster, David Greenberg is learning...

How to Survive Middle School

Donna Gephart

RATING: ★ ★ ★ ★ ★

I love creating characters, especially quirky characters. They feel real when they have faults and imperfections, dreams and desires. I have a long checklist of details about characters—age, family, school, secrets, etc. In fact, I teach a workshop about creating quirky characters. I tell participants that getting to know your character comes in layers—the surface stuff, like how she looks, then things she cares about, her experiences, and finally how she'd react in a really challenging situation. Names for characters are everywhere—baby name sites, playbills, obituary notices, even pet name books. Have fun with it and make sure the sound of your character's name matches the personality. Creating quirky characters is like getting to know a new friend.

TRY IT

Brainstorm a list of names that seem to fit certain personality types. What would be a good name for a boy who always loses things? A girl who wants to join the school football team? What about a really tough kid? A particularly nosy neighbor? Brainstorm names for characters (no fair using names of real people you know!), and then compare notes with your classmates to see if they agree.

WHAT NAME WOULD YOU GIVE A . . . ?	IDEAS FOR NAMES
Girl who wants to play football	
Boy who loses things	
Tough kid	
Nosy neighbor	
Mean teacher	
Funny teacher	
Clumsy girl	
Glamorous movie star	
Evil criminal	

Watt Key

Albert Watkins Key Jr., publishing under the name Watt Key, is an award-winning Southern fiction author. He grew up and currently lives in Alabama with his wife and family. Watt spent much of his childhood hunting and fishing the forests of Alabama, which inspired his debut novel, *Alabama Moon* (2006). His second novel, *Dirt Road Home*, was published in 2010. You can find him online at www.wattkey.com.

Most of my characters are built through dialogue. That's what I'm most comfortable with.

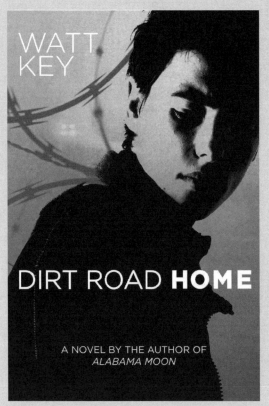

WATT KEY

DIRT ROAD **HOME**

A NOVEL BY THE AUTHOR OF
ALABAMA MOON

TRY IT

Dialogue, when a character speaks in his or her own words, reveals a lot about who that character is. Revising dialogue can be a great way to improve character development and consistency throughout the story.

Think about how your character would really talk. What slang might he or she use? Does the character tend to speak in long sentences or short ones? Find all of your main character's dialogue (words in quotes) and copy and paste just that dialogue into a separate document. If you're writing on paper, you can simply highlight it with a marker or colored pencil. Now read just your character's dialogue out loud. Does it sound consistent? Does it sound like the same person talking? If there are lines that don't work well, try out different versions to make the dialogue sound more natural.

Revision is like kung-fu.
Pain, discipline, patience,
and humility are needed
before you can go around
knocking people out with
your No-Shadow, Crane-
Style Fiction of Fury!

—TOM ANGLEBERGER

CHAPTER 10

Whose Voice Is It Anyway?

One of my favorite stories about writing has to do with voice.

Before I was an author or a teacher, I spent seven years as a TV news reporter and producer, starting out with a part-time job at the NBC affiliate in Syracuse, New York. I hadn't even graduated from Syracuse University when I was hired; I was unpolished and inexperienced.

One of the news anchors was an amazing writer but also a particularly grumpy, brusque guy. He didn't have much patience with beginners, and he was the person to whom I had to give my scripts for approval before they went on the air during the evening news. More often than not when I slid a story onto his desk, he would look down, skim through it, grunt, crumple it up, and toss it into the garbage can as if he were shooting a basketball. Then he'd write it over. His version was always better.

One day, I'd written a longer story for which I'd be recording the narration, and I was sure that my script would pass muster. Surly News Anchor didn't throw my work out, as usual, but he scowled at it.

"What is this?" he asked me.

Was it a trick question? "It's my news story," I said.

He shook his head. "This isn't you. Who are you trying to sound like here?"

"Well . . ." He had me there! There was an investigative reporter at a competing news station whose work I admired. I had written this particular story the way I thought she would write it, with that great, hard-hitting tone. So I told Surly News Anchor, "I was trying to sound like Sheryl Nathans."

"Well, there's your first problem," he said. "The job of being Sheryl Nathans is taken. By Sheryl Nathans." He handed the paper back to me. "You need to find your own voice."

Those words stayed with me through my journalism career, and I carried the same message into my English classroom and shared it with students (more gently and never with crumpled papers!). That advice has guided my life as an author as well. I believe that reading a wide variety of texts is one of the best things we can do to improve as writers, but I also know that at the end of the day, while I might learn about pacing from Suzanne Collins's Hunger Games trilogy or world-building from J. K. Rowling and Harry Potter or character development and research from Laurie Halse Anderson's historical novels, the voice of my writing can only be my own.

A Unique Voice

How do we help kids develop that unique voice? It can be a challenge, especially when standardized testing prompts seem to encourage what I call robot writing—give the main idea, support with details from the text, and summarize—and leave little room for creative voice. When that robot voice seeps into my students' everyday writing, I find that encouraging them to read aloud during the revision process is the best possible remedy.

Reading out loud—even if it's just in a soft voice so no one else can hear—forces a writer to hear the words he or she actually wrote instead of thinking the words he or she meant to write. If a student is writing in that robotic voice, reading aloud makes it apparent. In those situations, I often ask kids to put down their papers and simply tell me the story of what they were trying to say in the writing. The words that come out of their mouths represent that more authentic voice, and I'll repeat a sentence or two to show them. "That's what you just told me," I'll say. "That's what you should try to write now—in those words. *Your* words."

Sometimes, revising for voice means capturing the excitement that made you want to write about a topic in the first place. Susan Goodman, who writes nonfiction for young people, found she needed to revisit that earlier sense of passion when she was writing about scientists working on the ice cap in the Arctic.

She'd been lucky enough to fly up to the Arctic with the U.S. Air Force to spend time with those researchers, but later she found that when she sat down to write about the topic at home, everything felt flat. That robot voice was creeping into her manuscript. "Finally, I realized that I was trying to fit in so many facts that I had lost sight of what my book was really about—the excitement of exploration," Goodman says. "I had gone on a trip few people have experienced. I got into a plane that pulled up its landing gear when we took off from New York and lowered its skis when we landed a few hundred miles from the North Pole. I entered a world so cold that a cup of hot water, thrown into the air, would explode into a cloud of ice particles. So I sat down at my computer with an imaginary nine-year-old kid beside me. And I simply told that kid an adventure story—one where scientists were the explorers. I had found my voice."

When it comes to writing fiction in a character's point of view, author Nora Raleigh Baskin says developing empathy for that character is the key to making sure the voice rings true. "You have to be able to let go and be that person," she says, "even if it feels embarrassing or difficult . . . especially then. That is the best writing."

Patterns of Speech

Authors also need to know how a character might speak. Greg Leitich Smith, the author of *Ninjas, Piranhas, and Galileo* (2003), says reading his work aloud has helped him to develop his own voice. "At each draft, I will reread, both to see if it makes sense globally, but also for voice. . . . Really, it's just a sense of knowing the character and having an 'ear' for the language. I'm not really sure how else to describe it—it's sort of like being able to tell when a violin is out of tune."

Sometimes, eavesdropping can be a good strategy to help writers develop that authentic voice. Just how do real people talk? Author Sarah Albee says she listens to kids a lot. "I listen to their dialogue. I watch the way they interact with one another, and I channel myself at their age. If a character feels flat, I go back and revise, revise, revise."

Students can do the same thing. Is the voice of an adult in the story not quite real? Give kids the fun assignment of eavesdropping on actual adults. Encourage them to listen to the grown-ups at the dinner table and take notes on the kinds of things they say, their inflections and repetitive patterns. It's a great strategy for figuring out how to make a voice in writing more authentic.

Who's Telling the Story?

Revising for voice also means figuring out the best way to tell a story. Do you want to write in third person with an omniscient narrator who can see inside everyone's minds and hearts? Or do you want to tell the story in first person, through the eyes of one particular character? Authors often experiment with different points of view, depending on the story and its needs.

For example, I started writing *The Brilliant Fall of Gianna Z.* in third person, with an outside narrator telling the story, but somehow, the characters weren't coming to life the way I'd hoped. Rewriting in Gianna's point of view, channeling her creative, sometimes scattered personality, allowed me to add a whole new element to the story and help readers connect with her. Even then, my editor noted places where the voice didn't seem to match the emotion of what was happening in the story, like the situation where Gianna had lost the leaves she needed for class (see Figure 10.1).

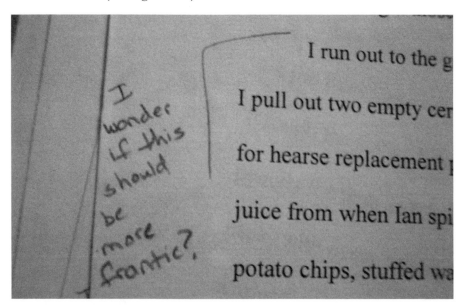

FIGURE 10.1
Editor Mary Kate asks a question about Gianna's emotional state.

Sugar and Ice was different. I'd written only a few pages in first person before I realized that it was the wrong point of view for this particular story. In order for readers to "see" Claire's growth as a skater, I needed to be able to describe her skating in detail, something that Claire couldn't do as a first-person narrator. So I changed *Sugar and Ice* to a close third-person point of view, from Claire's perspective but not in her actual voice. The reader is in her head—and only in her head—but the story is still told in third person.

Which Point of View?

Which point of view is the best for a particular piece of writing? Authors discuss the benefits and limits of first and third person. Many agree the best way to find the right voice is to simply try out the various styles, writing a few pages in each point of view to see which one works best.

I've been more at home with an omniscient point of view that allows me to see the world through every character, including the invisible narrator. Omniscient allows the narrator to be a character, the overseer. I like that.

—KATHI APPELT, AUTHOR OF *KEEPER* AND *THE UNDERNEATH*

First person is the same as dialogue. The narrator is telling you their story and they should tell it the way they talk. So get to know your character and let them talk. I like to let a narrator start a paragraph with the word *anyway*, the same way a lot of people do when they talk. It gets things rolling and you can always erase the *anyway* later.

—TOM ANGLEBERGER, AUTHOR OF *THE STRANGE CASE OF ORIGAMI YODA*

I write in first person quite often, because I find that it does help me to get into the mind of the character and make him or her come alive in my mind. But it can also be restricting: you the writer might have a beautiful, detailed bit of prose to describe a lovely flower garden the characters are walking through, but if your main character isn't the poetic type and doesn't know daffodils from dandelions, then you'll probably have to leave that description out.

—DEVA FAGAN, AUTHOR OF *THE MAGICAL MISADVENTURES OF PRUNELLA BOGTHISTLE*

The most important thing about writing in first person is realizing that your character's mind is the landscape you're exploring and that nothing can ever happen outside of that. You can't describe a thing the character didn't personally experience without some reasonable explanation that they read about it, had it described to them, or otherwise learned about it afterward.

—GREG FISHBONE, AUTHOR OF *THE PENGUINS OF DOOM*

The major thing to watch out for when writing in first person is not to get too drawn into a character's entire psychological world. We don't want to hear everything the character is thinking—that would be boring and just an overload of information.

—TANYA LEE STONE, AUTHOR OF *ALMOST ASTRONAUTS*

Writing in first person is sometimes tricky. Especially if you're creating a world that your reader might not be familiar with. You can't describe everything in that world because it's there all the time so the character who's speaking would take these things for granted. So I try to describe things that are important to the main character.

—NAN MARINO, AUTHOR OF *NEIL ARMSTRONG IS MY UNCLE & OTHER LIES MUSCLE MAN MCGINTY TOLD ME*

What matters to the main character in a story? I like to use an activity that connects setting to character to help my students figure that out.

The premise is simple: We go outside or to a window, depending on the weather (see Figure 10.2). We take in the scene in front of us and write about it three times. First, students write as themselves. What do they see, hear, feel, and smell? What do they notice about the weather, the landscape, the people, and the things in their line of sight?

FIGURE 10.2
Students stand at the window, recording setting details through a character's eyes.

Then I pass out character prompts, giving each student a character that he or she must become for the next writing activity (see Figure 10.3).

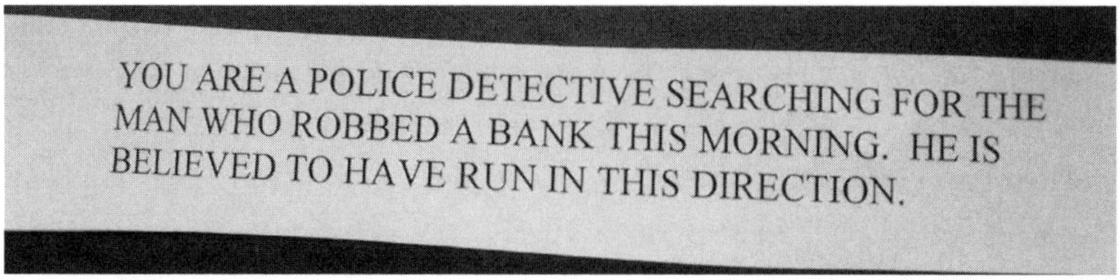

> YOU ARE A POLICE DETECTIVE SEARCHING FOR THE
> MAN WHO ROBBED A BANK THIS MORNING. HE IS
> BELIEVED TO HAVE RUN IN THIS DIRECTION.

FIGURE 10.3

An example of a student character prompt

For example, one student might be assigned the role of an elderly man who'd been widowed recently. Another might become a bank robber, looking for a place to hide stolen cash. A third might be a four-year-old child hoping to play outside that afternoon. Next, students take a few minutes to write about the outdoor setting again, this time in the voice of their assigned character. I ask them to pay attention to the person's situation as it relates to the setting. What would be important to the child? To the bank robber? How might the widower feel about the rain, compared to someone else?

Finally, I ask students to write about the setting, assuming the perspective of the main characters in their pieces of writing. What's going on in the character's world? What might be important to him or her? What kind of mood is he or she in? All of these considerations affect the voice of a piece of writing, and this "setting practice" can help students get used to writing in a particular character's voice.

Kathryn Erskine

Kathryn Erskine, a lawyer-turned-author, grew up in six countries, an experience that helps her view life and her writing from different perspectives. Her novels include *Quaking* (2007), an ALA Top Ten Quick Pick for Reluctant Young Adult Readers; *Mockingbird* (2010), winner of the National Book Award for Young People's Literature; and *The Absolute Value of Mike* (2011). Kathryn is a writing instructor and frequent workshop presenter. Her Web site is www.kathrynerskine.com.

To be sure I channel the characters' voices, I try to get into their heads and take a moment to be sure I'm that character. I might talk like them or wear their clothes (literally). When I was stuck on Matt in Quaking, *I put on a shawl like the one she is given in the story. When I got stuck on Caitlin in* Mockingbird, *I put my head under the sofa cushion to see how she felt.*

mockingbird
(mok'ing-bûrd)

Kathryn Erskine

TRY IT

What can you do to feel more like your character? How can you get into that person's head? If you're home and you have the right clothing (like the shawl Kathryn Erskine used to feel more like her character), then give it a try and see if it helps you get into that mind-set. Even if you can't dress as your character, you can always journal and talk as your character. Try writing in your character's voice in response to the following prompt. When you're done, read what you've written aloud, using your character's voice and expression.

The thing that really bugs me the most is _____

_____

_____

_____

_____

_____

_____

_____

_____

_____

_____

_____

_____

_____

_____

_____

_____

_____

_____

_____

_____

_____

_____

_____

_____

Suzanne Selfors

Saving Juliet (2008) and *Smells Like Dog* (2010) are among the many books that Suzanne Selfors has written for kids and teens. Her books have earned starred reviews, been chosen as Junior Library Guild and Indie Pick selections, and appeared on numerous lists. Disney studios has options on one of her books. She lives on a rainy island in the Pacific Northwest. Her Web site is www.suzanneselfors.com.

Voice is everything. It's the difference between a good book and a great book. This is when outside readers, trusted readers, can be extremely helpful to the writer during the early stages. My teen novel, Mad Love, began its life in third person. My writing group didn't feel connected to the story after they'd read it, and I couldn't figure out why I was feeling the same way. Once I changed to first person, the story took on a new energy. It was a nightmare changing the point of view on the entire manuscript, but it saved the story. It's an easy exercise to take the first page of the story and write it from one character's point of view, then write it from another point of view. Each version will have its own energy. Which version is most interesting? Most exciting? That's the version you want!

Smells Like Dog

by Suzanne Selfors

TRY IT

Take a scene or page from your manuscript and rewrite it in one or more different points of view. Is it written in third person? Try telling it in first person. Is it written in first person? Try switching to third, or use first person but let a different character be the narrator. Read your new versions aloud along with your original. Which one works best?

Revision is like my
mother's Indian cooking
because she relies on
intuition, experience,
and her own taste buds
instead of step-by-step
menus.

—MITALI PERKINS

CHAPTER 11

The Words We Choose

Because revision is a process, sometimes it helps to compare it to one with which students are more familiar, like making cookies. I often tell students that the big-picture revision jobs, such as dealing with organization and adding details, are the main ingredients in the dough. They're essential; no cookie recipe or, in this case, piece of writing, would turn out right without them. But if we're honest, we will admit that the flour and eggs are not what we love most about cookies; the chocolate chips are what really make us smile.

In the world of writing, surprising and vivid words and phrases are the chocolate chips. Once we take care of the theme, the plot, the research, or the character development, it's time to slow down and add those tastier nuggets, the moments that will make readers sigh with satisfaction.

When I'm revising a novel, I like to do a separate revision pass looking only at word choice. This slow-moving phase involves reading aloud, looking at each phrase, and making sure the words I've chosen are the best ones for the job. Sometimes my editors and I find places where the language just doesn't quite match the scene (see Figure 11.1).

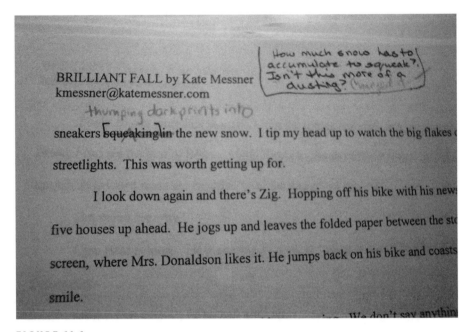

FIGURE 11.1

A note from my editor on the manuscript for *The Brilliant Fall of Gianna Z.*

But usually, my word-choice revision pass is about making the language more vivid, the nouns more concrete and tangible, and the verbs stronger, more active and descriptive.

For me, it makes sense to work on this part of the revision process after the bigger issues like time lines and themes have been addressed. Many authors feel this way; they need to assemble the skeleton of a book—make sure the bones are solid—before they can fine-tune the language.

Suzanne Selfors, author of *Smells Like Dog* (2010), says her revision process has overlapping pieces. "For example, right now I'm working on a first draft, and I have no idea what the landscape of this new world looks like. I'm not going to worry about it. That will come later, when I go back and begin to layer in the details. One layer will focus on inner dialogue, another layer might be all about what the characters look like, then another layer will bring the landscape to life. Layer after layer, gradually adding in the details. If I focused on these details in the first draft, the story would get nowhere, fast."

The Right Turn of Phrase

Selecting the right word is like sifting through a box of gems. In the right light, they might all look splendid. But which one is most suitable for this occasion?

As they refine their word choices, authors make it a point to give each word special attention. "I try to remember to write with nouns and to make every word count," says Deborah Wiles, author of *Countdown* (2010) and *Each Little Bird That Sings* (2005), "to use specific, concrete language . . . all tips from *The Elements of Style* that serve me well."

Reading writing out loud is a tried-and-true author strategy—one that's easy for kids to use, too. "Rich words jump out, and flat, stale ones do, too," says Rose Kent, the author of *Rocky Road* (2010). "I read out loud to myself and others and see which sections get people's eyes to light up and which make them fidgety. I think time and reflection are required to come up with just the right words."

How do we know which words are best and which should be saved for another day? The following guidelines can help students as they revise for word choice:

- Make general nouns more specific. When I talk about this concept with my students, I ask them to picture a dog, a particular breed of dog so there's a photograph in their heads. Then I read them this sentence. "The dog jumped into my lap." I ask them to close their eyes and imagine the scene. Some laugh. Then I ask them to open their eyes and tell me what kind of dog they saw. Inevitably, the answers vary greatly. "A Great Dane!" "A Chihuahua!" "A pit bull!" "A poodle!"

   I remind them to use specific language whenever possible. There's a big difference between a Great Dane and a Chihuahua (especially when it is jumping into your lap!).

- Get rid of adverbs when you can. Strong verbs are more powerful on their own. Don't say he walked quickly. Say he raced, half galloped, or scurried.

- Make your language more precise. Green comes in a thousand hues. Is it the green of an old bruise? The new, yellow green of spring leaves? The dull, muted green of pea soup?

- Don't be afraid to make up words. This can be especially vivid (and fun!) with sounds. Is the wind making a whoosh-whoo noise? Or a whistling rustle-grass sound?
- Watch for repetition. If you've used the word *walked* three times in one paragraph, try to find a way to get rid of two of them. Replace them with synonyms that are more descriptive or find a way to rephrase.
- Look out for clichés. Don't let your characters be quick as rabbits, quiet as mice, brave as lions, or anything else that's been overused. Come up with original comparisons of your own instead.
- Watch for tired body language. Do your characters nod or sigh on every page? Are they constantly rolling their eyes? Mix it up to avoid falling into this writing rut.

I shared one of my early drafts of *The Brilliant Fall of Gianna Z.* with some seventh-grade girls so I could get their thoughts on which parts of the book were working well. One of their comments on the manuscript made me laugh.

"TOO MUCH BLUSHING!"

Apparently, I'd gone overboard in trying to show that Gianna's feelings about her guy friend Zig were starting to change. I'd fallen victim to using the same tired words to describe that feeling of awkwardness.

My daughter gave me a similar comment when she was reading a suspenseful chapter of my middle-grades mystery, *The Star Spangled Setup*.

"I like this part, but too many things are giving Anna goose bumps."

She was right. I needed some new ways to show fear without resorting to the old goose bump cliché.

"My books are peopled with bobbleheads in early drafts," says Saundra Mitchell, author of *Shadowed Summer* (2009), who knows that she tends to let her characters nod their heads way too often. Part of her revision strategy is going back to change that body language and mix things up.

The Language of Emotion

How else can writers show what a character is feeling? In my creative writing classes, I sometimes use a partner activity to expand students' emotional vocabulary. I ask them to consider what we might do—other than smiling—when we're happy or excited. They start with a list of words that describe how characters might be feeling:

Angry
Sad
Upset
Happy
Excited
Afraid
Embarrassed
Worried
Focused

One student starts in the role-playing seat while the other takes notes. The role-playing student takes a minute to imagine a situation that would fill her with that particular emotion and acts out the feeling with her face and body. The other student writes like crazy, jotting down everything he observes or hears from the role-playing student. (See Figure 11.2.) What does the student's face look like? What are her eyes doing? What about the mouth? The muscles in her hands? How else is that student moving?

After spending a minute or two with each feeling, the students change roles. Each writer leaves with a list of "cliché-busters"—a notebook page full

FIGURE 11.2
Students role-playing feelings

of ideas for how characters might show feeling that go well beyond the usual nodding and blushing.

Revising Is Like . . .

Similes, metaphors, personification, and other poetic devices can also help bring writing to life during the revision process, as long as they're used sparingly.

"I use similes and metaphors like a carpenter uses a hammer—when it's the best tool to get the job done," says Donna Gephart, author of *How to Survive Middle School* (2010).

Eric Luper, who wrote *Jeremy Bender Vs. the Cupcake Cadets* (2011), agrees. "Similes and metaphors are devices I use a lot, but I'm very careful to stay away from clichés. If I don't have a zinger of a metaphor, I don't tread there."

Other authors feel more strongly about the tendency to overindulge in comparative and figurative language. "I think similes and metaphors should be illegal," says Tom Angleberger, author of *The Strange Case of Origami Yoda* (2010), "or at least you should need a permit to use them."

It is easy for young writers to go overboard when using poetic devices. Billy Collins has a delightfully funny poem about this issue. In "Litany" (from *Nine Horses*, 2002), Collins shares a thinly veiled warning about the judicious use of metaphors. "You are the bread and the knife," the poet begins, and then goes on to compare his beloved to everything from the "fish under the bridge" to "the pigeon on the general's head," in a playful mockery of overwrought poetic devices. Students love to laugh at Collins's satirical verse because it so clearly illustrates the metaphor-mania that good writers want to avoid.

MENTOR AUTHOR STUDY

Another great way to teach the use of similes and metaphors is by studying the work of a mentor author. When my seventh-grade classes were reading *Chains* (2008) by Laurie Halse Anderson, we spent twenty minutes one day focusing on her use of poetic devices.

Students worked in heterogeneously grouped teams of four, with copies of the novel, markers, and a big sheet of construction paper divided into three columns (see Figures 11.3 and 11.4).

FIGURE 11.3

Students collaborate on a mentor author activity.

FIGURE 11.4

Students search for examples of similes, metaphors, and personification in *Chains*.

Similes	Metaphors	Personification

Students had fifteen minutes to find as many examples of these poetic devices as possible. They recorded them in the correct column, noting the page numbers so students could go back to see the context later on. The result was a greater awareness of how a skilled author makes use of poetic devices that fit not only the time period of the work but also the characters' voices. Through this activity, Laurie Halse Anderson served as an unofficial mentor to my students and gave them models to follow as they worked to revise their own writing.

When it comes to revision, word choice lives somewhere between the big-picture issues and the nitty-gritty parts of editing, such as copyediting. Students can often write perfectly coherent papers without spending much time on this stage of the revision process. However, truly strong word choice is one of the things that separates good writing from great writing; it's well worth our time to teach these strategies for revision. So often, choosing just the right word makes all the difference.

MEET MENTOR AUTHOR

Deva Fagan

Deva Fagan lives with her husband and her dog in an old house with brightly painted walls. She writes fantasy and science fiction for teens and tweens. Her books include *Circus Galacticus* (2011) and *The Magical Misadventures of Prunella Bogthistle* (2010). Visit her Web site at devafagan.com.

I usually write in a point-of-view that is tied to a specific character (either first person or a tight third-person perspective). So when I am thinking about details and description, it helps me to think about my character, and what she or he would notice, and how whatever it is I am describing makes that character feel emotionally. For example, if the character is traveling through a forest: Is she scared, noticing the dark shadows where things might be hiding and feeling the oppressive height of the trees? Is she overcome by the beauty, noticing the bright green moss and birdsong? Or is she practical, noticing the edible berries and good camping spots?

Likewise, I try to make sure any similes and metaphors fit the point-of-view character's worldview and the setting of the book. So if it's taking place in a medieval setting, there's no "rumbling like a freight train." On the other hand, if the character is a physicist she might feel like "her stomach was contracting as if she'd just swallowed a black hole" when she's nervous. I usually put off heavy-duty revising for word choice until the later stages of my revision, however. It doesn't make sense for me to polish the descriptions of a chapter if I might end up cutting it out entirely because it doesn't advance the plot.

156

TRY IT

How might different people in different moods view your classroom? Try the following writing exercise to find out.

First, write as yourself. Look around the classroom and see what details you notice.

_____

_____

_____

_____

Now try writing as your teacher. What might stand out to you? What might you notice that the student missed? What would be more important to you?

_____

_____

_____

_____

Now imagine you are a time traveler, visiting from the year 1800. What would you notice first? And how would you describe this place?

_____

_____

_____

_____

Jeannine Atkins

Jeannine Atkins is a professor of children's literature at the University of Massachusetts and the author of several books for kids, including *Mary Anning and the Sea Dragon* (1999), *Girls Who Looked Under Rocks* (2000), and her latest, *Borrowed Names: Poems about Laura Ingalls Wilder, Madam C. J. Walker, Marie Curie, and Their Daughters* (2010). Visit Jeannine at her Web site: www.jeannineatkins.com.

I try to find the concrete details that I love and structure the poems around them. If I can I let them speak—if a window becomes more than a window, or looks a little like a book. Is a girl trying to keep something out or let something in? I can play with the concrete window and then it starts to have a different layer to it, so I really get a lot from my words, and I feel like they're speaking to the inside as well as the outside.

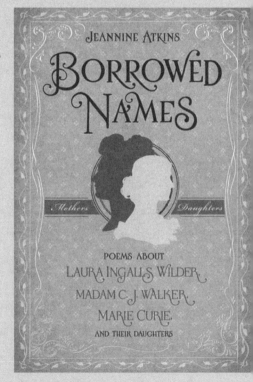

Jeannine Atkins tries to use concrete nouns—specific, precise words—and verbs that really suggest action. Need some practice being precise with your language? Try to replace the underlined general, vague words in the sentences below with more specific, vivid language.

Old: The <u>dog</u> <u>jumped</u> into my lap.

New: _____

_____

_____

_____

Old: My mom made me <u>clean up</u> the <u>junk</u> on my bedroom floor.

New: _____

_____

_____

_____

Old: When I <u>walked</u> into the house, I could smell <u>food</u> cooking.

New: _____

_____

_____

_____

MEET MENTOR AUTHOR

Mitali Perkins

Mitali Perkins was born in Kolkata, India, and im-migrated to the States with her family when she was seven years old. She writes fiction about growing up between cultures as well as books set in South Asia, including *Bamboo People* (2010) and *Rickshaw Girl* (2007). Visit her Web site at www.mitaliperkins.com.

I do a revision to make the writing more vivid and beautiful. That's my favorite and second-to-last revision.

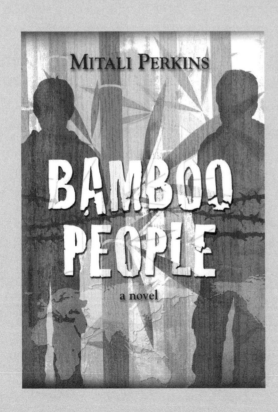

TRY IT

Once you've finished making all the big-picture revisions to a piece of writing, print out a copy and do a new read-through with a highlighter in your hand. Whenever you find language that's plain—words and phrases that could be more lively or beautiful—highlight it in the text. Then use a pen or pencil to write in possible word choices that are more vivid, and make those revisions in your next draft.

If you're working on a computer, you can use the highlighter feature in Microsoft Word to mark those words and phrases that could be stronger. Then use the comments feature (see Chapter 16) to make notes about words you might choose as replacements.

Revision is like cleaning your room because it may not be fun while you're doing it but when you're finished, you can stand back and see what you've done, and think, "Wow! That looks great!"

—LISA SCHROEDER

CHAPTER 12

Cut! Cut! Cut!

When I'm revising a novel, I almost always complete a separate revision pass with an imaginary chain saw in my hands. What can be cut to make this story move along more quickly? Sometimes, it's a word here or there. Sometimes, it's a bunch of dialogue tags—places where I've followed dialogue with a "he said" or "she said" when those words could just as easily be left out. Sometimes, it's people—characters who aren't really necessary to the story—and I go through page by page, erasing their lives until it's as if they never existed at all. And sometimes, it's entire scenes and chapters that I like but that don't move the story forward.

For example, my forthcoming dystopian tornado book, *Eye of the Storm* (2012), is an exciting story, and I knew the pacing in that book would be important to keep readers eagerly turning pages. So I spent a lot of time cutting scenes and words that slowed things down. What did my chain saw hack? Here's a sampling of what I deleted during just one week of revision:

- Dr. William Noyes. He was a secondary character whose job was already being performed by another, more interesting secondary character. Did I really need two scientists running the summer camp? No. Dr. Noyes had to go.
- A lot of getting-from-one-place-to-another scenes. When I'm drafting, I often feel the need to take every step of every journey with my characters. In this book, they were having a picnic in the woods, and when I wrote that scene the first time, I needed to step over every pinecone with them, hold back every branch, and feel every squish of every sneaker as they

walked to the spot where they were going to eat their sandwiches. I think that helped me mentally get to the place where the action happened, but my readers don't need (or want) to take so long getting there. I shortened this scene a lot when I revised.

- The word *actually*—about a thousand instances of overuse.
- The phrase *what looked like*. Reading through the manuscript, I found frequent sentences like this: She had what looked like jam all over her fingers. Really? If she's sitting there with toast, can't we just make the leap and call it jam? Delete.
- Most of Chapter 5 and Chapter 9. Don't worry. You'll never miss them. These were scenes where I was learning about the characters and exploring their setting in my mind, a journey that was important for me as an author, but one that doesn't need to be so long and drawn out for a reader.

How to Trim the Fat

Cutting sentences, scenes, characters, and unnecessary dialogue or facts should be part of the process when students are revising writing. How do writers know what to cut? Consider some of these frequent offenders.

SCENES WHERE IT TAKES TOO LONG FOR THE ACTION TO HAPPEN

My picnic-in-the-woods scene from *Eye of the Storm* isn't unique in the world of first drafts. Many authors find that they tend to write a blow-by-blow account of a character's day in early drafts, only to go back later and take out all but the most important elements.

Author Deborah Wiles had to revise with this in mind when she was working on *Countdown* (2010). "I went through so many steps to show how Franny put a slice of cheese into each biscuit just before it was finished baking," Wiles recalls. "I took pains to describe folding a cheese slice in fourths, then described how Franny took the biscuits out of the oven, opened them slightly with a knife, slipped a quarter slice of cheese into them, closed them, and slid them back into the oven to melt the cheese. My editor wrote me a note on the manuscript: 'I think we can just assume she put the cheese in the biscuits.'"

Like Wiles, students will sometimes need to streamline a particular section of text to keep the reader from getting bored. A good strategy is to have students go through a wordy first draft with a highlighter or colored pencil, marking everything that is essential to the text. Those highlighted phrases get to stay, while the rest gets chipped away to create a tighter, more focused next draft.

SCENES AND CHARACTERS THAT JUST DON'T FIT

Sometimes as authors, we include a scene or a description or a character simply because it means something special to us, and that makes it easy to ignore the fact that it might not fit the story we're trying to tell. When I turned in *The Brilliant Fall of Gianna Z.* to my editor, the chapter where Gianna and her friend Zig go hiking in the mountains to collect leaves was a lot longer. It included a scene where Gianna pauses to think about a hollow tree in the middle of the trail, and she tells Zig a story about how she used to hide in it when she was little; one time she fell down and started rolling down the mountain until her father caught her and picked her back up.

My editor sent a note back on the manuscript asking if that whole scene could be cut; she didn't think it advanced the story. My first reaction was "No! I love that scene!" Because the truth is, that wasn't Gianna's hollow tree. It was mine.

My son's very first hike was a small Adirondack peak called Rattlesnake Mountain, and in the middle of the trail was (you guessed it) a hollow tree where he liked to play as a toddler. He did indeed start rolling down the hill one day until my husband scooped him back up. My editor was right. I liked the story a lot because it was personal, but it had nothing to do with Gianna and Zig. I cut it out of the book. (But note that all is not lost when a favorite scene needs to be cut from a particular draft. I found a way to tell the story in a different piece of writing: this one!)

Ask just about any author about cutting scenes from a manuscript, and most likely, he or she will remember a favorite page or paragraph that simply had to go. In Kathryn Erskine's *Mockingbird* (2010), it was Caitlin's Sunday school scenes. "They weren't really necessary for the plot," she says. "They were funny and related to the plot but didn't add enough to make them necessary, so I cut them."

"I cut scenes all the time," says author Watt Key, "mostly those that don't progress the story. In *Alabama Moon*, there was a scene where Moon and Kit waited out a bad lightning storm in the trees. I loved the scene, but eventually cut it because it was just dragging out the boys in the wilderness too long." Key says he tends to include too many characters in a first draft, so some of them have to go.

Author Kirby Larson eliminated a character while she was revising her Newbery Honor Book *Hattie Big Sky* (2006). She says her editor helped her see that the change was necessary. "She saved me from including a character—one I adored!—who saved Hattie's bacon every time she got in trouble. Because I loved Hattie so much, I didn't want anything bad to happen to her, but in protecting her, I was weakening the story. I am so grateful to Michelle Poploff for encouraging me to 'dump' Ned."

Kathi Appelt emphasized how difficult it can be to let go of a favorite character. "The main character in *The Underneath* was originally a boy who rescued a cat from a tree. For several drafts, this boy and his family played a major role in the story. One day my agent, Holly McGhee, told me that she thought that whole story strand needed to come out. We were talking about a hundred pages of text!" Appelt says. "At first I resisted, especially because that boy very closely resembled my oldest son. But once I started removing the strand, I realized that she was exactly right. That part of the story had given me the real story and it had served its purpose. Was it hard to remove? Yes. But it was the right call."

Like many authors, Danette Haworth initially resists recommendations to part with a section she's worked hard to create. "I hate when parts of the book don't fit in!" says the author of *The Summer of Moonlight Secrets* (2010). "I once had to cut a scene that featured a room the characters never entered again. The room was scary and full of cobwebs, and I loved it! That's what blinded me to its relevance. It took the eyes of another writer to see it, and once she pointed it out to me, I knew it had to go. But I didn't delete it entirely. For every manuscript I work on, I create a scrap file; that's where I save chunks of text I love but can't use. Who knows? Something in those passages might be useful in the future."

Students also may balk at deleting a section of text that took them time to write. Suggest that they save the omissions in a "maybe someday" file. Knowing that they can come back to a favorite scene, character, or phrase can keep them from feeling like they've wasted time.

REPETITION

Readers are smart. Once you've told them something, you generally don't need to repeat it. Yet as authors, many of us do fall into this trap in our early drafts. Reading aloud is a great way to discover unnecessary repetition. Other times, you may need a second set of eyes to see the patterns. My editor caught one of my stuck-in-the-same-groove recordings (see Figure 12.1), but having students read one another's drafts during the revision process, paying special attention to repetition, can accomplish the same goal.

FIGURE 12.1

A note from my editor helps avoid repetition in the story.

Author Loree Griffin Burns knows that she needs to watch for repetition when she revises her works of nonfiction. "I find that during the drafting stage, I often repeat paragraphs or descriptions in multiple places," she says. "This usually means that I've not quite figured out the best way to include certain information, so part of my revision process becomes figuring out where the information fits best."

Other authors of nonfiction for kids agree that trimming excess verbiage can sharpen their stories. "And cutting can often happen to me at a very late stage in the game," says Tanya Lee Stone. "There was an entire chapter in *The*

Good, the Bad, and the Barbie that was flipped on its head and had more than half cut out of it in order to tighten its focus and make it more interesting."

Students can take this advice to heart when they're writing research papers and other works of nonfiction as well. The idea is not necessarily to include everything they learned in their research (a tempting option, since it took so long to take all those notes!) but to craft a piece of writing that is interesting, informative, and cohesive. Sometimes that means leaving some of those details and facts from their notes out of the final draft.

When author Jim Murphy finished his first draft of *The Crossing* (2010), the text was 270 pages with an additional thirty-five pages of notes and sources. "It was way too long," Murphy says, "and I knew it. . . . But how to cut a very complicated text about George Washington's first year as commander of the American forces without killing the tone and pace of the text? My editor suggested I hold a tighter focus on George Washington, so I went back over a hard copy of the text and highlighted every direct discussion of George in red ink. Then I went to the computer and deleted everything except those sections. (It was painful to cut so much text, especially since it was pretty good, but I knew it had to be done.) Then I set about stitching what remained together, going through my usual revision process numerous times."

What to Cut: Authors Share Their Personal Hit Lists

On the large scale, I will try to cut any scene that doesn't contain some sort of change: The main character learns something new, or faces some new challenge, or comes to some decision. On a smaller scale, I try to cut words or phrases that are just repeating something that is already there.

—**DEVA FAGAN, AUTHOR OF *THE MAGICAL MISADVENTURES OF PRUNELLA BOGTHISTLE***

I just love to use *just*. It's just so natural to just write and write and just let the words just flow, you know? I weed most of those *justs* out in revision.

—**LINDA URBAN, AUTHOR OF *A CROOKED KIND OF PERFECT***

In large revision, I try to cut extraneous material. I ask myself, "Is this necessary?" if I find myself with a lot of exposition or narration. I also ascribe to the domino theory— *each* scene must topple into the next and make that scene topple into the next, etc. If it doesn't do its work, it can go, no matter how beautiful it is.

In small revision, I look for wordiness and sloppy writing. I am forever removing gerunds ("ing") and strengthening my prose that way. . . . "He went sailing over the fence" is stronger as "He sailed over the fence . . ." It's small, but it makes a difference, especially when applied to the entire story.

—DEBORAH WILES, AUTHOR OF *COUNTDOWN*

I have a few little rules. Never more than one metaphor per page. Never use the same word in the same sentence (other than common words). Try not to use the same word in the same paragraph, and maybe not the whole book. And if you can't find a new way to express something (avoid clichés at all costs) then just say it straight, i.e., "She was crying."

—NORA RALEIGH BASKIN, AUTHOR OF *ANYTHING BUT TYPICAL*

The Words on the Post Office Wall: Most Wanted

While individual writers have "pet" words that they tend to overuse, some words can almost always be cut from a piece of writing. Here's a list of the frequent offenders—words and phrases that tend to make text weak and nonspecific.

- It looked like/It seemed like

These phrases can often be eliminated, making the statement stronger.

Instead of:

It looked like her mother was getting ready to go to work.

Try:

Her mother was getting ready to go to work.

Or better yet:

Her mother rushed around the kitchen, stuffing her briefcase with papers and folders for work.

- I said/he said/she said

Often, dialogue tags can be eliminated altogether or replaced with a sentence about what a character is doing as he or she talks.

Instead of:

"I can't wait until the guests arrive," Heidi said.

Try:

"I can't wait until the guests arrive." Heidi pulled the chocolate chip cookies from the oven.

- Adverbs

One writer told me she's known as a serial killer of adverbs during the revision process. How come? Adverbs—words that modify verbs—tend to make writing weak and sometimes awkward. Strong, active, vivid verbs create richer images in a reader's mind.

Instead of:

"Get over here!" she said loudly.

Try:

"Get over here!" she screamed.

Instead of:

She knocked loudly on the door.

Try:

She pounded on the door.

Instead of:

He walked casually over to my desk.

Try:

He sauntered over to my desk.

MORE WORDS FROM THE WRITER'S MOST-WANTED LIST

just	in that moment
and	so
rather	a bit
began to	I guess
as though	maybe
then	that
but	very
always	really
glanced	

Pruning Makes a Tree Stronger

Just like trimming certain branches from a tree can strengthen it, cutting extra words from a text can make it stronger. Sometimes, to help my seventh-grade writers focus on a particular aspect of revision, I have them move from table to table in timed increments, with different tasks and materials at each table (see Figure 12.2).

FIGURE 12.2

With a model to follow on the whiteboard, students move from table to table, working on different revision tasks.

In our personal narrative unit, for example, students visit one table where they use orange sticky notes to add bits of description. At another table, they use pink ones to mark opportunities for dialogue. At another, they mark weak word choices with a yellow highlighter, and finally, they spend time at the table with the orange highlighters to identify words that should probably be cut.

I model all of these activities with my own personal narrative on the whiteboard before they start, and students are always surprised at just how many words can be cut from my paragraphs without losing meaning. They help me mark throwaway words—*just, really, very*—and phrases that are irrelevant to the story. Then we read it again, and they notice how the stronger words—those active verbs and vivid nouns—are able to shine once the fat is trimmed away.

When Brittany took the time to read her personal narrative at the "What to Cut" table (see Figures 12.3 and 12.4), she noted words and phrases that were unnecessary, marked them for deletion, and discovered a tighter, stronger draft living within her first story.

FIGURE 12.3
Brittany works to identify dead weight in her personal narrative.

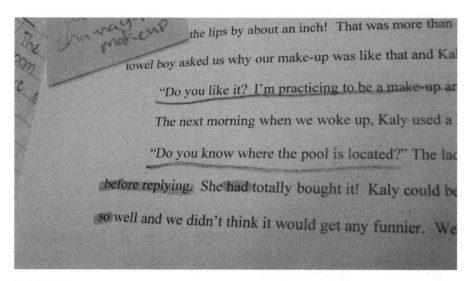

FIGURE 12.4

Words that might be cut in the next draft are highlighted.

Overwriting tends to be more of an issue for adults than it does for young writers, particularly when it comes to those who aren't excited to put words on the page to begin with. But reluctant writers, too, need to cut words and phrases from their writing sometimes. One way to help them is to return to the heart of the piece of writing.

What job is this piece supposed to do? If it's sharing a story, then irrelevant details should be targeted when it's time to make cuts, and these can be replaced with more description about the elements of the story that are important.

What about persuasive writing? If the goal is to persuade, every sentence in the essay or letter needs to work toward that goal. There's no room for random details or, worse yet, facts that serve to contradict the argument the author is trying to make. Encourage students to cut these and replace them with additional evidence to support their opinions.

No matter the genre, sometimes less is more. It's like pruning that tree. Eliminating the dead weight of unhealthy branches or unnecessary words is important. Getting rid of words and phrases that aren't working hard makes room for new growth—new ideas and details that will make the whole piece stronger.

Olugbemisola Rhuday-Perkovich

Olugbemisola Rhuday-Perkovich was the "new kid" at school many times over, in more than one country, and currently lives with her family in Brooklyn, New York, where she loves walking and working on crafts in many forms. Her middle-grades debut novel, *8th Grade Superzero* (2010), received a starred review from *Publisher's Weekly* and was named one of Amazon's Best Books of the Month. She holds a master's degree in education and a Professional Development Certificate from the Teachers College Reading and Writing Project at Columbia University. Olugbemisola enjoys incorporating her different ways of working and playing into author visits and workshops. She is a member of the Society of Children's Book Writers and Illustrators, a PEN Associate Member, and a former Echoing Green Foundation Fellow. Her Web site is www.olugbemisola.com.

Having conversations with an editor is invaluable, especially when I have to fight for something—I have to make sure that it's worth fighting for, that there are genuine character/story reasons to keep something.

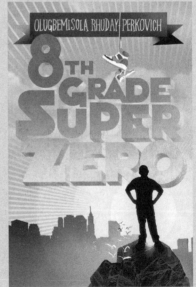

TRY IT

Put your sentences on trial. When it's time to cut words, phrases, and sentences (maybe even whole paragraphs and pages) from your piece of writing, you need to be tough. Olugbemisola Rhuday-Perkovich's question about whether a particular passage is worth fighting for can bring the importance into greater focus. What would happen if you deleted the sentence or paragraph? Would the piece of writing still make sense? Would it be as vivid, quirky, or entertaining? What role does the passage play in your piece?

Imagine that you're standing before a judge who has put your sentences on trial. Your job is to defend them, to go through your story line by line and explain why each sentence must stay. You might find that you can advocate for some sentences but not others. Keep the best and send the others off to be deleted.

Revision is like exercise because it keeps your writing muscles strong and your storytelling sensibilities in shape for the game (or race or book) ahead!

—LOREE GRIFFIN BURNS

CHAPTER 13

Talking It Out

Ask students to identify their favorite things about school, and most will probably include "friends." Kids love to talk to each other. Sometimes we have to corral the conversations in the classroom, but other times we want to capitalize on students' enthusiasm for communication. Encouraging students to collaborate on writing goals and talk about the craft of writing can motivate rather than deter them from revising.

You probably realize that by the time you pick up a book in a store or library, the story has taken a long journey from the author's imagination to the printed or digital page. What you might not realize is how many people traveled on that journey. Start with the acknowledgments section if you want to trace some of the helping hands. Authors typically give credit to the people who have guided their books along the way—from the research, through that long revision process, and on through the editing and design.

Jane Yolen, who published her 300th book recently, believes in talking about her writing with friends. For thirty-five years she has worked with a critique group, whose members have won many writing awards. Yolen spends four months a year in Scotland, and frequently consults a critique partner there as well.

"When I read something aloud in my writers' group, I often hear the problems even before anyone else tells me," she says. After her critique group helps her revise, Yolen's editors chime in with their thoughts. "Recently, an editor had me change the newly married point-of-view young woman in my new picture book *Elsie's Bird* [2010] to a child whose mother had just died. And she was so right! Now the book sings."

Jody Feldman's opening scene for *The Seventh Level* (2010) benefited from her critique partner's feedback. "I began the book with Travis on top of his school, about to retrieve an important cap that was stuck to the bricks between the second story and the roof," Feldman says. "One of my critiquers pointed out that if I started the story a few minutes earlier, that would give my readers a chance to learn a little about Travis, which would, in turn, make them care about him more. That ultimately let me learn more about him and made him a richer character."

Tom Angleberger, author of *The Strange Case of Origami Yoda* (2010), says his next book, *Horton Halfpott* (2011), has been passed from reader to reader, improving each time. "First my wife, author/illustrator Cece Bell, read it and told me a tough truth—it was confusing. I rewrote it to clear up the plot and the unfolding of events," he says. Then an editor asked for deeper characters. "So, in addition to many other changes, I took two 'snooping stable boys' and gave them the dream of someday becoming butlers. This really gave me something to work with—especially with dialogue. . . . After I had been through that book so many times, there was still room to tell the story better, and I needed her help to find it. The point is, I was too easily satisfied and thought I was done each time."

As teachers, we've all encountered students who completed a draft and thought they were finished with writing. By introducing a social element into the revision process, we can give them an incentive to revisit and review their writing.

A Small Circle of Writer Friends

Writing groups take many forms. Some members meet in person over coffee and brownies once or twice a month. In these sessions, writers may take turns reading stories and passages out loud, often distributing copies so others can read along silently and take notes or provide reflections in the margins. This is a model that I use quite often in my creative writing class (see Figure 13.1).

FIGURE 13.1
Toni and Emilie discuss a manuscript.

We designate certain days as critique sessions, and students know they'll be sharing a page or two of their writing when they come to class. They arrive with copies to distribute. Students sometimes choose a passage they especially like, but just as often they choose scenes that have vexed them for one reason or another. They may ask their classmates to listen with a focus question in mind. Does a certain character feel real? Is an exciting scene tense enough, or has it become bogged down by description?

During one of our sessions, Addison asked for help with the setting of her story. She was in the process of switching from the modern day to America's pioneer days. Her critique partners listened respectfully, complimented her on her character development, and then kindly pointed out that she had left the telephone and refrigerator in the narrative when she backtracked a full century. Addison left the session with a good feeling about her decision to shift the setting but also with fresh insights about how to revise to make the historical scene more authentic.

A Safe Space to Talk About Writing

I think it's essential to model the respectful language that we expect students to use when commenting on one another's work. I typically share the following guidelines with my students:

- Start with the positive. Begin by commenting on an element of the writing that you think works well or a section you especially like. I show them how Mary Kate, my editor at Walker/Bloomsbury, begins her revision letters by telling me how much she loves my book and then gets into her suggestions to make my writing stronger. (See Figure 13.2.)

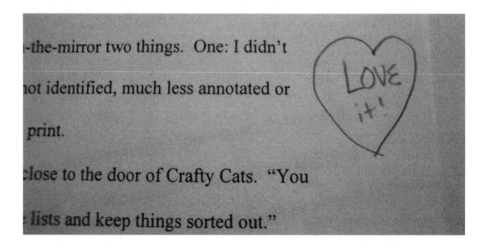

FIGURE 13.2

Mary Kate notes a section of *The Brilliant Fall of Gianna Z.* that she thinks is working well.

Like student writers, authors need to know that the person reading their work is on their side. Such support makes us more willing to work hard on the suggestions for improving later on.

- Ask questions. A good question can stimulate and clarify a writer's thinking. After the discussion, the writer will have an easier time expressing those ideas on the page.
- Make suggestions, but use language that makes it clear the writer owns the words. For example, instead of saying, "You need more detail here," a

critique partner might say, "Do you want to elaborate on that so readers get a really clear picture?" Instead of saying, "Need to add conflict here," try asking, "Did you consider letting the girls have an argument over this? It seems like a good place to introduce their differences."

- Don't sweat the small stuff. In critique sessions that are focused on revision, try not to get caught up in smaller editing concerns. If you keep looking for the spelling errors, you will likely miss the bigger picture.

Whether the group consists of seventh graders sitting at their desks in class or published authors meeting over coffee and manuscripts, the goal is the same: to make the writing stronger.

Sometimes writer friends need to push one another beyond their comfort zones. Deborah Wiles, the author of *Countdown* (2010) and numerous other novels for young readers, discovered her tendency to leave out difficult scenes. "I don't realize I do this until my editor catches me," she says. "For instance, in *Love, Ruby Lavender*, I didn't write the scene when Ruby watches her grandmother leave for Hawaii. 'You need that scene,' said my editor. She was right. I wrote it. In *Countdown*, I didn't write the scene where JFK talks to the nation about the Cuban Missile Crisis and Franny's family watches it together. 'I think the reader needs this scene, in order to feel the horror that Franny feels,' said my editor. He was right. I wrote it. It made a big difference."

Author Danette Haworth relies on her editor to let her know when she's left something out. Just because an idea is obvious to the writer doesn't mean it will be to the reader. In *Me and Jack* (2011), the father of the main character is an air force recruiter during the Vietnam War. Haworth knew how stressful his job must have been, but she didn't include that in the story because it seemed obvious . . . until her editor asked why the father was angry all the time. "I was surprised!" Haworth said. "I didn't envision the father as angry, nor did I want him viewed that way. So I went back into the manuscript and included those close moments between Joshua and the dad, the humorous moments." She also added scenes where the boy witnesses some antimilitary behavior and develops a better understanding of his father's emotions.

Sometimes, a new point of view is just what a writer needs to solve a persistent plot problem. Julie Berry had revised Chapter 15 of *The Amaranth Enchantment* (2009) four times and just couldn't get it right. The scene in question required her main character to both fall in love with a boy and steal something that she needed from his pocket. Ultimately, Berry says, it was her husband who came up with the solution in one of their talk sessions. What if the item was in the boy's coat pocket? And what if the boy lent the girl his coat because she was cold? Berry loved that solution; it gave her main character perfect access to the boy's pockets!

Sometimes, sharing work with another reader confirms a problem that a writer already suspects but may not be ready to accept. "My outside readers help me by verifying what I often already feel about a piece," says Loree Griffin Burns. "For example, in my first draft of *Tracking Trash*, I was unhappy with the final chapter. It was not a satisfying ending. I had convinced myself that it could work, though, and sent it to my editor anyway. When she wrote back and said, 'This doesn't work,' I knew I had to go back to work."

Students should also know that a critique group serves another important role—encouraging a writer who's lost his or her way or simply run out of steam. Author Kathryn Erskine says she is indebted to a friend who wouldn't accept that she "wasn't in the mood" to write. "She finally said, 'Stop making excuses. Sit down and write!' I did, and I finished the book!"

Writer Liza Martz had taken a long break from writing books but regularly posted blog entries about her volunteer work with animal rescue groups when one of her critique partners, Loree Griffin Burns, prompted her to get moving on a new project. "Loree wrote this comment on one of my blog posts: 'Goodness, Liza, could you do a book? I think you should take your passion for animals and rescue work and found an entire genre of children's literature.' That encouragement got Martz thinking. "I checked out my blog and was stunned. Somewhere along the way I had found the perfect subject matter for a book. Even better, I'd found my voice!" She got started on a new nonfiction project that same week.

Students can provide that same kind of support for writers, that same mix of complimenting, questioning, and suggesting, either through a classroom discussion or electronic communications.

Many authors have critique groups that meet mostly online. My own writers' group operates that way; it's made up of Loree and Liza from the story above, as well as Eric Luper. We have a Yahoo group set up where we post manuscripts when we'd like feedback from other members. When someone shares a chapter or a whole manuscript, the rest of us go online, download the document, and use the comments feature on Microsoft Word to share our thoughts (see Figure 13.3).

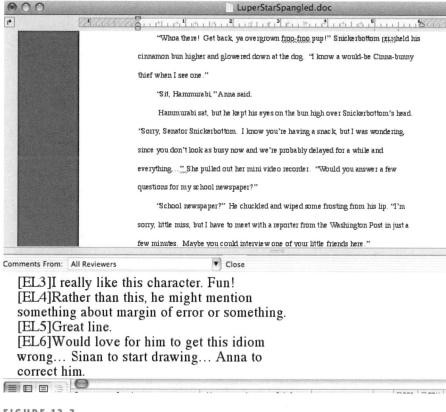

FIGURE 13.3

Eric Luper comments on an early draft of *The Star Spangled Setup*.

I've made use of this same feature when conducting student critique sessions in the computer lab. Students save their finished drafts and either e-mail them to a friend or simply switch computers so they can read each other's work. Then the critique partner uses the comments feature to provide the same sort of feedback that's offered in our class critique discussions (see Figure 13.4).

How to Use the Comment Feature in Microsoft Word

Note: These directions are for Word for Mac and will vary, depending on your operating system and the version of software you use.

- Use your mouse to highlight the text that you wish to discuss.
- Go to *Insert* at the top of the screen and select *Comment* from the drop-down menu.
- Your comment will be added to the manuscript. In order to see it, the original writer simply needs to choose the *View Comments* option when he or she gets the document back.

This is a great strategy for what I like to call "Reluctant Revisers" because the list of comments turns into a simple to-do list. Students can check off the comments as they address them and have a real sense of accomplishment.

In a revision-friendly classroom, you also might want to consider having students choose specialties—areas of expertise for which they might be especially helpful revision partners.

"Some authors I know are great with humor," says Olugbemisola Rhuday-Perkovich, the author of *8th Grade Superzero*. "Some are very plot oriented, etc. That helps me take a closer look at specific areas or elements."

When I submit a manuscript to my critique group, I know that I can expect different kinds of feedback from different readers. I count on Eric to let me know what can be cut—he's a stickler for getting rid of extra words and streamlining language. I look to Liza to question the places where my logic doesn't quite connect, and I know that Loree will take a long, hard look at the characters and let me know when their actions don't match their personalities and motivations.

Throughout the school year, you and your students might discover each other's special powers. Who can always find a place to add humor? Who's a careful researcher who can suggest a better source or a crisper argument? Who has a knack for inviting leads and intriguing introductions? Who's good at sweeping out the word clutter? Who can spot inconsistencies in a time line? Who's the crusader for stronger characterization, someone who knows how to round out an imaginary person's features? Keep a classroom list of your writing specialists and post it for everyone to reference during the revision phase.

When students become classroom experts, they take ownership of the revision process and of their own learning. As teachers, we become facilitators, setting the stage for conversations about writing with instruction and discussion time. It won't be quiet—and it may not always be pretty—but students who talk about writing often end up with more ideas, more strategies, and more enthusiasm for revision.

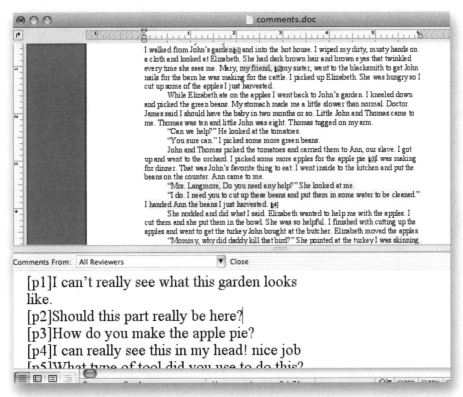

FIGURE 13.4

A seventh grader leaves comments on a classmate's personal narrative.

Talking It Out: Revising a Graphic Novel

The Babymouse series includes a great deal of art with the text, so author Jennifer Holm and her brother, illustrator Matthew Holm (see Figure 13.5), have many conversations before the projects get to the final draft stage. Figures 13.6 through 13.10 show what their collaborative revision process looks like, from *Babymouse: Queen of the World!* (2005).

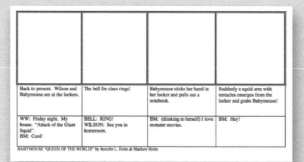

Back to present. Wilson and Babymouse are at the lockers.	The bell for class rings!	Babymouse sticks her hand in her locker and pulls out a notebook.	Suddenly a squid arm with tentacles emerges from the locker and grabs Babymouse!
WW: Friday night. My house. "Attack of the Giant Squid". BM: Cool!	BELL: RING! WILSON: See you in homeroom.	BM: (thinking to herself) I love monster movies.	BM: Hey!

BABYMOUSE "QUEEN OF THE WORLD!" by Jennifer L. Holm & Matthew Holm

FIGURE 13.6 — An early outline for two pages of *Babymouse: Queen of the World!*

FIGURE 13.7 — Early sketches for the spread

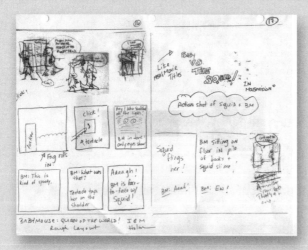

FIGURE 13.8 — A more detailed sketch and layout

FIGURE 13.9 — Another step closer to the final draft

FIGURE 13.10 — The finished spread from *Babymouse: Queen of the World!*

Rebecca Stead

Rebecca Stead is the author of *When You Reach Me* (2009), a New York Times best seller and Notable Book and winner of the 2010 Newbery Medal. Rebecca's first novel for children, *First Light* (2007), is a Junior Library Guild selection and one of Bank Street College of Education's Best Children's Books of the Year (2008). Rebecca grew up in New York City, where she worked as a public defender for many years. She lives on the Upper West Side of Manhattan with her husband, Sean, and their sons, Jack and Eli. Her Web site is www.rebeccasteadbooks.com.

Rebecca Stead shared the following thoughts in a May 2009 interview with *School Library Journal* blogger Elizabeth Bird.

These questions were trickling in: How could Miranda have known X? But if that's what happened, then wouldn't Z logically follow? Why did Q? What happened to F?

And one day I just lost my sense of the book's internal logic. I had this sudden horrible certainty that the whole thing could never stand up. I remember being in my bedroom and experiencing a wave of nausea. And I called my dad, who is the person who introduced me to science fiction when I was a kid, and watched lots of Star Trek with me, and who has this great way of enjoying speculative fiction and taking it very seriously at the same time.

I asked him to meet me. In an hour, if possible. I hadn't told him anything at all about the book yet, so we sat in a restaurant and ordered breakfast and I laid out the whole story, all the pieces. And when I got to the end he was making this very weird scrunched-up face. I said, "What's wrong?" And he said, "Nothing's wrong. I'm trying not to cry."

When he said that, I thought, okay, I have to make this story hold together somehow. So we just sat there and talked until I had a handle on it again. And when I got that back, I knew immediately which parts of the book didn't fit, and how to answer all the questions I'd gotten from our readers. And continuity was never a problem after that.

TRY IT

Sit down with a partner and explain—without reading your piece of writing—what happens. You might notice that you can't easily summarize the story or the thesis or the message, a sure sign that the point isn't clear in your own mind. Time for some revision. If you are able to recount the story, then ask your listener if he or she has questions or lost interest along the way. Answering the questions and discussing your ideas can help you target the repairs.

Julie Berry

Julie Berry received an MFA in writing for children and young adults from Vermont College of Fine Arts. *The Amaranth Enchantment* (2009) was the second novel she wrote in school, and the first one to sell to a publisher. Since then she's written *Secondhand Charm* (2011) and the Splurch Academy for Disruptive Boys series with her older sister, Sally Faye Gardner, as the illustrator. Visit Julie's Web site: www.julieberrybooks.com.

Because it's frightening to cut, I sort of cut gradually. I take a look at something and think, "This might be superfluous," and so I'll put a strike-through on it, in [Microsoft] Word, which is a formatting choice that blocks it out. So then it's gone, but it's not really gone. Then I can reread again and think, "How do I feel now with this tentatively gone?" It'll usually become clear to me that "This is better" or "No, I really need that," so it's this cautious process of seeing what I can do without.

TRY IT

Worried about eliminating your hard work in a piece of writing? Try Julie Berry's method of tentative cutting to take away the sting. If you're writing on a computer, use the strike-through feature (one of the choices under Format-Font-Effects in Microsoft Word) to see what your writing would be like without that phrase or sentence. Then, if you like the change, you can delete the text for good. If you're writing on paper, a light pencil line through the text in question is another great way to "try on" revisions before you actually start cutting.

Linda Urban

Linda Urban loved to write when she was growing up in Detroit. She is the author of the middle-grades novels *A Crooked Kind of Perfect* (2007) and *Hound Dog True* (2011) and the picture book *Mouse Was Mad* (2009). She lives in Vermont with her family, and you can visit her Web site at www.lindaurbanbooks.com.

I have an excellent editor in Jeannette Larson at Harcourt. Jeannette asks lots of questions, which get me to think through the logic of my characters. Here's an example of how: In A Crooked Kind of Perfect there is a scene in which my main character, Zoe, is given a gift by her friend, Wheeler. It is a piano-shaped cake topper, made out of marzipan. I was using that scene for mood and pacing: I needed a few happy moments before Zoe got some very bad news. On a sticky note Jeannette asked me: "Even if Wheeler is really talented, wouldn't this piano look like a kid made it? Do you think Zoe would comment on that?"

I read Jeannette's question and thought, well duh! Of course Zoe would notice, but she wouldn't care. All that would matter was that Wheeler made it for her and it would be perfect. Sure, it would be crooked, but to Zoe it would be a crooked kind of perfect.

Oh! Suddenly the entire theme of the book dropped right into my lap—as did the title, which I didn't have yet. I never would have gotten to that point without Jeannette's smart questions.

TRY IT

Questions that "critical" friends raise about our writing can be powerful revision tools. Trade papers with a partner, and grab a pen or colored pencil. Read your partner's manuscript and, in the margins, jot down questions that occur to you as you read. The questions can be simple ("Why would he do this?" or "What was she thinking when this happened?") or more complex ("If she's riding her bike to her friend's house for the party, how could she possibly carry that huge birthday present?"). Afterward, trade papers back and talk about the issues you each raised. Let the reader ask the questions while the author listens, thinks, and then answers. When it's your turn to listen and answer questions, be sure to have a notebook handy so you can remember ideas brought up during the discussion.

Karen Day

Karen Day lives in Newton, Massachusetts, with her husband and three children. After careers in journalism and teaching, she began writing middle-grades fiction. Day's first novel, *Tall Tales* (2007), was chosen as a "best book" by the Bank Street College of Education. Her other books include *No Cream Puffs* (2008) and *A Million Miles from Boston* (2011). Visit her online at www.klday.com.

KAREN DAY

A Million Miles from Boston

For me, revising means putting on different editing hats. Sometimes I'm an editor who only looks at different threads. Sometimes I'm an editor who skims through, looking for chapters that are too long, paragraphs that are too long. Sometimes I'm an editor who cuts the details that don't have multiple means of furthering the plot or shedding light on my characters. But I can't do all of those jobs at the same time.

TRY IT

You can take Karen Day's advice literally and dig four or five different hats out of your closet if you'd like—but you can also use this strategy without putting anything special on your head. Make a list of "hats" you think you should probably wear to revise the particular piece of writing you're working on. Some examples of different kinds of writing and the editing hats you might want to wear as you revise them appear on the next two pages. The list includes specific things to look for on each revision pass for that genre.

FOR POETRY	FOR FICTION	FOR A RESEARCH PAPER
Noun-patrol hat: Are all the nouns in this poem specific and concrete?	*Character hat:* Do all the characters feel real, and do they act in ways that are consistent with their personalities?	*Fact-checking hat:* What details do you need to confirm to make sure they're accurate?
Verb-patrol hat: Are all the verbs in this poem active and descriptive?	*Setting-details hat:* Are there places where you could describe the setting in better detail?	*Plagiarism patrol hat:* Have you included phrases that are not in your own words? Be sure to attribute if you need to use a quote; otherwise, rewrite.
5-senses hat: Does the language in this poem appeal to all of the senses?	*Pacing-police hat:* Have you included scenes/ sentences that aren't essential? Would the story work better without them?	*Elaboration hat:* Are there ideas in this paper that haven't been fully explained? Mark them so you can add more detail and elaboration later on.
Extra-word hat: Get rid of every single word that's not doing an important job in the poem!	*Timekeeper's hat:* Do all of the events in the story follow a logical time line that makes sense from one page to the next? Can you put the events on a calendar?	*Organization hat:* Do the ideas that are grouped together make sense together? Is the report easy to follow, and does one idea lead naturally to the next?

FOR PERSUASIVE WRITING	FOR TEST WRITING
Thesis hat: Is the point of your writing clear from the beginning, and does the piece end by restating the same point?	*Question hat:* Have you answered all parts of the question? Underline the parts if it helps!
Prove-it hat: Are there many details and examples given to support each of the ideas put forth? Which ideas need more support?	*Examples hat:* Have you given specific examples from the text to support your ideas as needed? Can you add more?
Consistency hat: Does everything in this paper support the main argument? Are there any facts/details that seem to contradict it?	*Clarity hat:* Is your writing easy to understand? Can someone who's grading it quickly see that you've done the job you were asked to do?
Voice hat: Read out loud when you wear this hat. Does it sound like there's a real person behind the writing? How can you make it more conversational?	*Word-choice hat:* Where could you improve a word choice to make it more specific, more lively, or more vivid?

Revision is like military-style push-ups because it's hard and not all that fun, but there's a certain joy in doing it well and it definitely improves strength—both of the work and the writer.

—JONI SENSEL

CHAPTER 14

Clean Up: The Copyediting Process

Tell the truth. Some of you skipped right to this chapter, didn't you? I recognize you with your red pens. You became teachers at least in part because you always got perfect scores on the spelling tests, right? Run-on sentences make you cringe, and comma splices cause you to break out in hives. And right now, you're probably thinking, "Thank goodness she finally got around to talking about conventions!"

Well, here we are. Conventions do matter. But I'm still going to make a special appeal to save this editing process for last, after students have had a chance to focus on the content, ideas, organization, and language in their writing. How come? Because that way kids won't spend time working on text that's going to end up deleted anyway. Because they won't be able to make a few quick spelling corrections and think they're done. And because last is where this type of editing happens in the real world of writing books.

I wrote no fewer than thirteen drafts of *The Brilliant Fall of Gianna Z.* before the manuscript reached the copyeditor, the stage in the book-production process where a skilled reader goes through the manuscript with a real or electronic version of a red pencil, marking everything from typos to trademark infringements to make sure mistakes don't end up in the final book.

Although I was one of those perfect-spelling-test kids and am now an author and English teacher, I make writing errors that need to be corrected (see Figures

14.1 and 14.2). But if the publisher had forced me to fix the grammar gaffes as well as address the recommended content and stylistic changes in each of those thirteen drafts, I may not be a published author today.

Let me be clear: Writing conventions are an important part of the revision process—as long as they are not the first or the only changes we ask student writers to make.

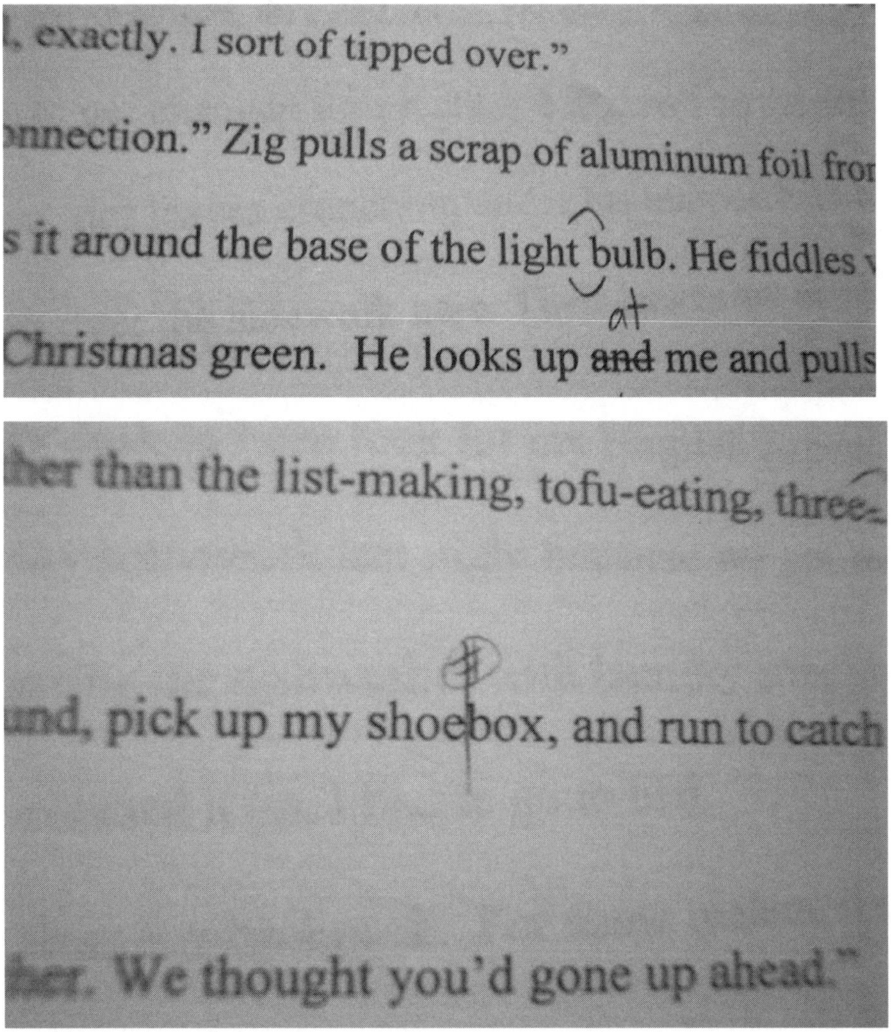

, exactly. I sort of tipped over."

nnection." Zig pulls a scrap of aluminum foil fron

s it around the base of the light bulb. He fiddles

Christmas green. He looks up ~~and~~ at me and pulls

er than the list-making, tofu-eating, three-

nd, pick up my shoebox, and run to catch

er. We thought you'd gone up ahead."

FIGURES 14.1 AND 14.2

Copyedits for *The Brilliant Fall of Gianna Z.*

Beyond Spelling and Punctuation

In the real world, the editing process involves so much more than checking spelling and punctuation. Nonfiction authors, in particular, depend on copyeditors to check their facts and search for inconsistencies.

Susan Goodman, author of *The Truth About Poop* (2004), credits a sharp copyeditor for saving her from a "great embarrassment" when she neglected to verify a tip from a tour guide at the U.S. Space and Rocket Center in Huntsville, Alabama. Told that disposable diapers had originally been invented for the astronauts, Susan couldn't wait to include the dirty details in the "Waste in Space" section of her book. "Luckily, not for long," she said. "My wonderful copyeditor sent me a citation about Marion Donovan, the mother who invented the disposable diaper in the early 1950s, long before the Gemini astronauts were donning their spacesuits or any other equipment. I felt quite sheepish that my mistake had slipped through, but I was grateful it had never made it into print."

Eric Luper, author of the historical novel *Bug Boy* (2009), said he was amazed and grateful for the level of precision in the final editing phase. "The copyeditor checked every reference, company, and figure of speech I used to make sure it was in existence in 1934, the year my novel took place," Eric said. "And boy, did she catch a lot of them."

Authors do a great deal of fact checking and editing on their own before a book makes it to the copyeditor, but that editor still plays an essential role. Sometimes, it takes a new set of eyes to catch mistakes that a writer who is so close to the product might miss.

Sometimes, when copyeditors aren't sure about a fact or detail in a text, they'll send a note to the author asking for verification, and the author will have to provide the source for the information.

This is a great activity for the classroom, too. Ask students to pair up to read over one another's papers, using colored pencils to underline any fact or detail that seems shaky. Then they can return the papers to the authors, who can run their own fact-checking session, confirming each of the questioned details and writing a quick note in the margin about its source. Students often discover an error in their note taking through this process, and many come to understand that "hearing it somewhere" is not a reliable source for nonfiction writing.

The Brain: A More Reliable Tool Than a Computer Spell-Checker

In the copyediting stage of revision, too many students have learned to rely on the computer spelling- and grammar-check functions, which are so full of problems that I can't begin to list them. While I'd never want to discourage students from using these software tools, I offer an editing lesson to help them understand that computer checks are just one editing device that should be used in conjunction with many other strategies.

Here's the editing checklist I give students when they're ready for this last stage of the writing process:

1. Read your paper out loud. Be sure to read carefully so that you're reading the words that are actually on the page, rather than the words you meant to write. Sometimes it helps to cover all but the line you're reading with a piece of paper, moving the paper to show the text line by line as you read. You'll probably find sentences that don't make sense. Some may have extra words or missing words. Stop to fix these while you're reading.

2. Read your paper out loud a second time to check for run-on sentences. If you get to a point where your voice wants to stop, but there's no punctuation on the page, stop and take a look. If it's a run-on sentence, fix it by breaking it into two sentences or combining the phrases into a compound sentence with a comma and conjunction or a semicolon. During this pass, you should also make sure each sentence begins with a capital letter and ends with the correct punctuation.

3. Read your paper a third time, checking for common spelling errors that you tend to make. Do you confuse *there*, *their*, and *they're*? Watch for those "spelling monsters," and feel free to look up words in a dictionary or ask for help if you're unsure.

4. Now run a computer spelling and grammar check to help you catch errors

that you might have missed before. Instead of taking all of the computer's suggestions, imagine it's a person sitting next to you and asking, "Hey, did you mean to say this?" Think about what the program is suggesting and make sure any suggested changes are really what you intended to say.

5. Have at least two friends read your paper, using a colored pencil or the comments feature on the computer software program to mark any errors you might have missed.

6. Return to your own paper or computer, make changes, and read through the draft one last time, making sure it represents your best work.

I encourage you to let students know that they have the final word on decisions about their writing. Not all of the suggested corrections may be necessary or even accurate. Everyone makes mistakes, after all, even professional copy editors. Author Greg Fishbone still laughs about one of those incidents. "In a friend's book, I've seen a copy editor turn 'poplar trees' into "popular trees," which, I guess, would be trees with a whole lot of Facebook friends."

And finally, tell your students not to worry if their drafts are covered in red marks during the editing process. Published authors make many, many mistakes in their books, too, most (but not all) of which are corrected before the book ends up in stores and libraries.

Tales from the Trenches: Authors Share Copyediting Stories (and Nightmares!)

It's embarrassing to get your copyedited pages back and they are covered in red! My main problem is I never know if a word is a compound or hyphenated. This was a constant problem in *Smells Like Dog.* Treasure-hunting or treasure hunting? Soup spoon vs. soupspoon? And you can't rely on your computer program to get it right. I'm so grateful for copyeditors! (Or is it copy editors?)

—**SUZANNE SELFORS, AUTHOR OF *SMELLS LIKE DOG***

Bamboo People has one typo in it involving clothing. It was caught by none other than Roger Sutton of the *Horn Book*, who pointed it out after reading the ARC [advanced reader copy] in the hopes we might be able to change it. But alas, it was too late! I don't want to talk about it. Lost sleep one night over it. I want the book to sell so that we can reprint a second edition with that mistake fixed.

—MITALI PERKINS, AUTHOR OF *BAMBOO PEOPLE*

Since *Chess Rumble* is told in urban dialect and there is no grammatically correct English in it, I had to create a dictionary of slang rules and exceptions. That device also helped me to realize that even street talk has absolute rules, and it made the voice even better. It was pretty funny to see a copyeditor call me on incorrect grammar because I'd make it too correct, violating my own rules!

—G. NERI, AUTHOR OF *CHESS RUMBLE*

When I was a picture book editor, I realized there is a practically unlimited number of ways you can mess up a picture book, be it in text, pictures, design—you name it. I've had apes in a monkey pen, seven beach balls on the number 8 page, even a book bound on the right, not the left (this was when I lived in a country where they read right to left). For *Poop Happened*, I had a few nights where I sat up straight in bed with a shock of horror, realizing I forgot to credit the Litchfield Historical Society for letting me photograph their chamber pot, or had misspelled Peloponnesian, and Harappan, and Ambroise Paré. . . . I had a picture of the wrong Henry IV to accompany a caption (there was a Henry IV of France and a Henry IV of England)—all caught before printing, but still, it's a stressful job, ours.

—SARAH ALBEE, AUTHOR OF *POOP HAPPENED! A HISTORY OF THE WORLD FROM THE BOTTOM UP*

Once my editor at Scholastic, Dianne Hess, called and said she was sending a copy of a new book's jacket for my approval. She was giggling when she told me this, so I knew something was up. Seems that when the designer put my picture on the back flap, she inadvertently used the photo of another Jim Murphy who published with Scholastic. And I'd met the designer several times, but I guess never made much of an impression with her! But I did like the cat the other Jim was holding and suggested they just stick my face over the other Jim's face to save money. They didn't do that, of course.

—JIM MURPHY, AUTHOR OF *THE CROSSING*

I remember writing once about how something shouldn't be "scene" when I meant "seen." I think often it's my subconscious speaking to me, though, because that scene was eventually cut. Obviously, it shouldn't have been "seen"!

—KATHRYN ERSKINE, AUTHOR OF *MOCKINGBIRD*

In *Kimchi & Calamari*, my character Joseph is an avid comic-book reader. He is talking about Superman once, and I mistakenly worded it so Joseph says Kryptonite gave Superman energy, when in fact, it is the opposite. Kryptonite destroys Superman. This would have been quite disturbing to all my comic-book-fan readers, and I was grateful when copyeditors caught my miswording.

—ROSE KENT, AUTHOR OF *KIMCHI & CALAMARI*

Revision is like a lottery
ticket because it's a golden
opportunity to make your
work even better!

—DONNA GEPHART

CHAPTER 15

What If the Writing Is Already Good?

O nce upon a time, I had a conversation with a young writer about a project she'd turned in to her teacher. It was a short story that she'd eventually have the chance to share aloud on a classroom performance day. It was a rough draft, she told me, but she hoped to revise it based on her teacher's comments before the sharing day.

But when I talked with her the following week, her demeanor was different.

"We got our papers back," she said.

"So you're ready to start revising?"

"No," she sighed. "All she wrote on it was 'good job.'"

I think this student must have been imagining something like the editorial letters that the UPS guy delivers to my house, detailing pages of revision suggestions from my editors. "Good job" was not what she'd had in mind.

"Well, maybe you could look at it again and sort of make your own revision suggestions," I offered.

She shook her head. "Nope. Because after she gave it to me with the good-job note, she took it back to keep it for Friday [sharing session], since it's ready."

I have no doubt that this was a teacher who spent countless hours making sure her lessons were appropriate and engaging for students. I'm sure she thought the compliment on the paper would make the student's day.

It didn't.

Revising for Excellence

That moment is one that has truly impacted my teaching life. How many times had I offered up a "good job" when what my gifted writers really wanted was a challenge? How many times had I handed out an A when what they really craved was constructive feedback? Sure, their writing is good. They know it's good. What they don't know is where to go from there. How do we handle the revision process for students who are already strong writers?

When I assign a major writing project, I try to have a due date before the final due date. At this stage I want to see where my young authors are in the writing process, and I want to provide appropriate feedback to every student. No matter how good a writer you are, there's always room to improve.

For students who are struggling, my feedback will include the usual suggestions—reading aloud to make sure ideas are clear, adding details, taking another look at organization. For those who already have a solid draft, I'll move into more advanced revision strategies—experimenting with the structure of a text, trying alternative beginnings and endings, fine-tuning word choice, and playing with voice.

Mentor Texts

Providing more advanced mentor texts enables students to see examples of higher-level writing. When I assign a persuasive writing piece, for instance, I'll generally give out a sample essay or letter to the editor that demonstrates the basic elements. Once my more advanced students have mastered that structure, I'll provide more sophisticated examples of the genres—opinion pieces from the *New York Times*, say, or *Newsweek*'s "My Turn" column. Spending time with these additional mentor texts lets students see not only the rules for this type of writing, but also that some rules can be broken effectively and selectively, that different moods can be created through the voice of a persuasive piece, and that strong words make a big impact.

Using mentor texts to guide gifted writers can be taken a step further with other genres. If students are interested in nonfiction, for example, we could steer them to exemplary works such as Loree Griffin Burns's *Tracking Trash*, Tanya Lee Stone's *Almost Astronauts*, and Jim Murphy's *An American Plague* to study the structures of these books. All are award-winning titles that capture students' interest as well as provide a how-to guide for writing narrative nonfiction.

We might suggest that students read interviews in which authors answer questions about their craft. What makes nonfiction writing clear, coherent, and compelling? How do good writers establish a sense of immediacy or place, particularly when they are referring to events from the past? What are effective strategies for organizing arguments or explaining complex processes within a narrative? Is it necessary to follow the traditional journalistic structure of who, what, when, where, why when writing informational articles, or are there other ways to provide essential details with a more original flow?

The same mentor-text analysis can work with fiction. Students interested in writing realistic fiction, for example, might choose authors whose work they admire and reread their novels with a writer's eye. How do those authors handle conflicts between characters? How do they deal with transitions and time passing? The rule among adult writers is that you should read at least a hundred books in the genre in which you'd like to write before you pick up a pencil or start typing. Introducing advanced writers to mentor texts and mentor authors gives them the same experiential base.

Revision Takes Many Forms

Some gifted students pose a different challenge when it comes to revision. Those who haven't been pushed to revise their already-good writing may be reluctant to "mess up" their tidy, perfectly spelled papers with notes. It's already good, right? Why scribble all over it?

For students in this camp, it helps to know ahead of time that revision will be part of the process, that a typed or neatly written draft isn't a final draft, but a starting place. That's a point my colleague Marjorie Light and I emphasize from the beginning in our seventh-grade Advanced Creative Writing elective. We write alongside our students on a daily basis, so they see our manuscripts in progress and watch us working on our good-but-could-be-better books. We share processes and strategies with our students. We make time to revise. And we practice flexibility.

For the work session shown in Figure 15.1, for example, we proclaim a step-back-to-plan day. Students have been in the computer lab the last few classes, making great progress on their works of fiction. We provide them with models for a return to the outlining process, whatever shape that process may take for individual writers. I show students how I use the Scrivener index-card feature to identify the scenes I need to write in a novel. Most don't have access to that software at home, so we use paper index cards in class, and students spread them out on the tables, sketching out where their stories will go from here.

FIGURE 15.1
Students in an advanced creative writing class try different revision strategies.

Students follow our directions and spend the rest of the period planning. However, when they return to continue working with the cards the next day, it's a different story. Instead of outlining on her index cards, PJ has her setting map out and is studying it. Lauren is scribbling symbols that I don't understand in the margins of her cards. Lee is rearranging hers as if she's playing poker with imaginary friends. Brianna is journaling on a separate piece of paper. And Serena has been staring into space with a little smile on her face for the past fifteen minutes or so.

What do these already-good writers need? Bossing them back to the index-card activity we had planned isn't the answer if we're to expect authentic, quality writing. Instead, I take a quick walk around and stop to conference with each student.

"So how's it going?"

I'm not sure who coined this question as the quintessential reader/writer conference phrase, but it works. Inevitably, students answer "Fine." When I pause and wait for more, they start thinking aloud, and I can see where they are in the revision process and get a better idea of what they might need.

PJ has reached a point where she's not sure where her story is going. She's taken out that map so she can review it, literally walking her characters through the landscape to see if that jars an idea for their next steps. She doesn't need intervention from me; she needs quiet time to finish doing that job, so I move on.

Lauren's index cards are marked with either triangles or stars. "The stars are the really big scenes, where something exciting happens," she explains. She's writing a dystopian book in which the world is facing catastrophic events as the main character is coming of age and falling in love, and she's wondering how to balance those two story lines. I grab a piece of blank paper to model an over-and-under time line that I've used in my own projects. It's a traditional time line with one story line mapped out above the dates and another mapped out below. She loves this idea, so I pull out a bigger sheet of construction paper, and she gets to work. When the period ends, she has a much better sense for how her two plot lines work together (see Figure 15.2).

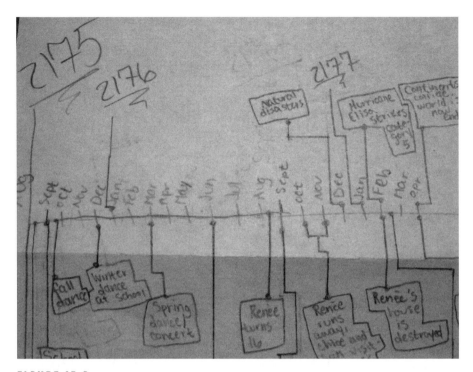

FIGURE 15.2
Lauren's "over-and-under" time line

Lee, who has been looking at the sequence of events in her futuristic story, tells me that she needs to figure out more about what the world is like. We have a quiet conversation about the concept of world-building, and I print off the six-page worksheet I designed when I was wrestling with the same issue for my dystopian novel.

By the end of the period, no one is doing what we'd originally planned, and this is just fine. They've moved on to their next steps, all different and tailored to their individual projects and writing styles.

Was the writing already good? Absolutely—but it's about to get even better.

Revision is like eating
potato chips because
sometimes you don't know
when to stop.

—SUZANNE SELFORS

CHAPTER 16

Technology Tools of the Trade

The good news: You can teach the revision strategies in this book with nothing more than paper and pencils.

The better news: If you're fortunate enough to have some technology available to you in the classroom, you can use it to make revision more efficient, more relevant, and more fun for your students.

Leaving Digital Comments

Chapter 13 discusses the use of Microsoft Word's comments feature as a tool for critiquing student writing, whether the reader is you or another student. It's a variation on the traditional "comments in the margin" strategy that I absolutely love. Once a draft of a document is complete and saved, students can e-mail it to you or a friend, upload it to a file-sharing area, or simply move from their computers to let someone else sit down to read. When readers wish to make comments, they simply highlight the text to which they're referring, click on *Insert* at the top of the screen, and select *Comment* from the pull-down menu. The process may vary for different operating systems and versions of Word.

A box will appear, with plenty of room for quick comments and questions or even whole paragraphs discussing that section of text. The reader goes through the entire document, making comments along the way, and then saves it. At this point, I think it's helpful to have students use the "Save As" command to render an entirely new version of the document. This ensures that the author's original work is saved and allows the writer to open both versions side by side to revise.

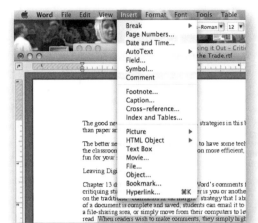

FIGURE 16.1

Using the Comment feature in Microsoft Word

To see the comments on the document, the writer needs to open it, click on *View* at the top of the screen, and scroll down to *Comments* on the pull-down menu. The reader's comments will appear either on the side or at the bottom of the screen, depending on the version of the software being used.

Comments can be "closed" after the writer has addressed them, or after he or she has decided not to address them. Remember that whether they come from you or from a classmate, suggestions are just that—suggestions—and ultimately the decision about how to best improve a piece of writing should rest with the author.

Don't Go It Alone

It's a big world out there, full of other teachers and authors who can help you encourage your students to revise. Why go it alone when technology makes these kinds of connections quicker and easier than ever? We've already discussed the topic of author mentors, and while your school may or may not be fortunate enough to fund in-person author visits during the school year, there are other ways your students can benefit from their expertise.

AUTHOR BLOGS

Many middle-grades authors write blogs as a way to keep in touch with their readers in between writing books, and some offer amazing glimpses into their writing processes. Check out the Web sites of authors with whom your students are familiar; many will include a link to a blog that's updated regularly, and you can bookmark these to share with your students. Kids love to hear the stories-behind-the-stories, the "secret" details of how a scene got cut out of a novel or how a title changed. It makes them feel like part of that writing world, and when they hear that authors are hard at work on revision—just like they are—it can be a powerful motivator.

Because revision is my favorite part of the writing process, I tend to blog about it a lot, and I use the tag "revision" to mark those blog entries so they're easy to find. Just do a quick search for "Kate Messner revision," and your search engine should return a handful of those focused blog entries.

If you bookmark author blogs or add them to your blog reader, you can accumulate quite a collection of useful links for the classroom. I like to keep these bookmarks in folders organized by topic. So whenever I find an author blogging about researching a new project, for example, I bookmark the blog entry and drag it into my research folder (copy and paste on a PC). Blog posts about word choice, or theme, or good beginnings go into those folders, and so on.

Please keep in mind that not all children's author blogs are entirely kid friendly. Some writers blog for an audience of other writers, mostly adults, so be sure to preview blogs before you share them with students. Ready to start collecting resources? Here are links to the blogs of some middle-grades authors who write frequent, kid-friendly posts about the writing process:

Loree Griffin Burns
   http://lgburns.livejournal.com

Sara Lewis Holmes
   http://saralewisholmes.blogspot.com

Cynthia Lord
   http://cynthialord.livejournal.com

Kerry Madden
   http://mountainmist.livejournal.com

Kate Messner
   www.katemessner.com/blog

Linda Urban
   http://lurban.livejournal.com

SKYPE CHATS: ALMOST LIKE BEING THERE

Skype author chats may be one of the fastest-growing ways to connect student writers with author mentors. Skype is free videoconferencing software that enables authors to make virtual visits to classrooms, libraries, and book clubs half a world away. It can be a cost-effective alternative to pricey, in-person author visits and still let students ask authors questions about everything from research to revision.

As a teacher-author-mom, I'm a particular fan of Skype visits because I can use them to interact with students around the globe (one of my Skype visits took me from my porch overlooking Lake Champlain to a classroom in Australia) without leaving home.

During my Skype chats with classes, I walk kids through the revision process of whichever one of my books they've read with their teacher ahead of time. Using the webcam on my computer, I show clear images of editorial letters, marked-up manuscripts, outlines, planning pages, and to-do lists (see Figure 16.2) so that by the time our twenty-minute chat has ended, students have a much better idea of the revision strategies that happened behind the scenes before that book appeared on a bookstore or library shelf.

FIGURE 16.2

Sharing a marked-up manuscript page with students via Skype

In the creative writing class I teach, we often call on particular authors to address specific revision issues. When one of my students was struggling with the next steps for the novel in verse that she was writing, we scheduled a Skype visit with author Lisa Schroeder, whose novels in verse are popular with my middle school girls. When we were focusing on revising our opening pages, we scheduled a chat with author Deva Fagan, who had just started work on a new project. She talked about how she works to make sure her openings are engaging and make the right promise to readers about what the rest of the book will be.

Like a regular author visit, the benefits of Skype author visits last long after the videoconference. As an author, I often receive e-mails from students many months after our Skype visit, letting me know that they tried out a particular revision strategy I'd suggested and telling me how it worked. As a teacher, I find myself saying things like, "Remember what Lisa told us about how she cuts extra words?" And my students nod. Long after our personal connections with authors, those mentor writers continue to inspire kids and get them working, revising.

TWITTER AS A REVISION TOOL

Some colleagues looked at me like I was nuts when I shared the news that I'd set up a Twitter account for my seventh-grade classes during the 2009–2010 school year. I had originally signed up for Twitter to make connections with other writers and to help market my novels. What I hadn't anticipated when I started tweeting was the network of educators I developed and the great ideas I'd get from them every day.

Just what is Twitter? It's a social networking site where users share ideas, links, and resources in 140-character "tweets," or updates. Twitter users "follow" each other and see their tweets on a single page that's updated in real time. The people I follow on Twitter (aside from my husband, who is a meteorologist, tweeting the weather) include a long list of writers, authors, librarians, and teachers. The result is a steady stream of book recommendations, teaching ideas, links to useful Web sites, and questions about books, writing, and teaching.

That's the other cool thing about Twitter. Once you've developed a network of followers and people you follow, you can go there for help. The other day, a student came into my classroom looking for a book. It was about a girl named Amy, she thought, "who went to school and was better at everything than

everybody else, and she found out she had come from this lab or something."
The librarian had no idea what book it was. Her teacher had no idea. And I had
no idea. So I turned to Twitter.

"Student is looking for a book w/ MC Amy who runs faster, swims better,
finds out she is part of lab experiment. Help?"

In less than two minutes, no fewer than five of my Twitter followers had
identified this book as part of the Replica series. I caught up with the student in
the library, and the librarian put in a request for an interlibrary loan for the book.

So what does this have to do with revision? One day when my creative
writing students were working on character development, we logged in to
our classroom Twitter account and posted this question: Writers, how do you
develop your characters?

By the time our class met the next day, we had responses from many writers
and authors, including some of my students' favorites (see Figure 16.3).

TWITTER REPLIES TO OUR QUESTION: HOW DO YOU DEVELOP CHARACTERS? 9/23/09

debbieduncan @MessnerEnglish To develop characters'
personalities, I sometimes take a classic archetype & tweak it.
I also empathize with my villain.
2:30 PM Sep 23rd from web in reply to MessnerEnglish

rebstead @MessnerEnglish I know writers who "interview"
their characters . . . I've never tried it, but am curious about
it.
2:16 PM Sep 23rd from web in reply to MessnerEnglish

SaraLewisHolmes @MessnerEnglish Character shines in
contrast: use a setting where the MC is not at ease, or make
'em meet their evil twin. :)
10:29 AM Sep 22nd from Tweetie in reply to MessnerEnglish

JeannineGarsee @MessnerEnglish I try to be careful not to let
my characters sound alike. Each needs to have their own
speech patterns, slang words, etc.
9:46 AM Sep 22nd from web in reply to MessnerEnglish

FIGURE 16.3
Author responses via Twitter

Later in the semester, the creative writing class noticed a problem that seemed to permeate all of their stories. Their characters were frowning and blushing and gasping too much. The invasion of the tired body language had hit their manuscripts hard, and they weren't sure how to fix it. If you're embarrassed and you're not blushing, just what are you doing?

We turned to Twitter for ideas. After letting followers of our classroom account know that we were tackling the problem of tired body language, we sent out a series of tweets.

"Other than blushing, what might you look like if you were embarrassed?"

"Other than getting goose bumps, what might happen to you if you were scared?"

"Other than smiling, what might you do if you were happy?"

Almost immediately, we started getting replies. Students opened their notebooks, made a page for each emotion, and made lists of what "scared" might look like, what a character who is embarrassed might be feeling.

Those pages filled out their toolbox for revising clichéd body language, and Twitter became one of our go-to resources for expanding our writing community beyond the walls of the classroom.

Revision is like a dog...
no wait, rewriting is like a
mongrel beast, no I got it,
revising is like a Siamese
cat! Because no, despite,
wait, for it's cross-eyed
and never stops purring...
oh I give up!
Writing is rewriting.
Period.

—G. NERI

CHAPTER 17

The Revision Classroom, Revisited

B y now, you probably feel like you're buried under a mound of sticky notes and marked-up manuscripts. After all this talk about adding comments and interviewing characters, taking online field trips, adding details, and conferring with author mentors, what might our classrooms look and sound like on revision days? How can all this be put into action? It all comes down to five key ideas.

Make Time

A piece of writing that's completed in one hour, or even one that's assigned one day and due the next, is not going to be revised in a meaningful way. In the age of standardized tests, short (and, let's face it, superficial) writing is a reality in our students' lives, and we can explain to them that certain kinds of writing need to be done without much revision, sometimes without any revision at all. But if we value quality writing, we also need to make time for revision.

Whether for fifteen minutes every day or half an hour every week, try to schedule revision periods as part of your classroom routine. Once students know that revising is important enough for you to make time for it, they'll begin to recognize the value to the writing process, too.

And give students time to think. Remember that revision, by its very defini-tion, involves seeing something again, and we can't do that if we've never looked away in the first place. Consider making some pieces of writing longer-term projects, and give students a break between the draft writing and the revision so that they have the chance to see anew.

Create a Revision-Friendly Environment

You don't need to rent a lakeside inn, but do consider making your classroom a place that's friendly to the revision process. That means room to spread out. It means having access to the kinds of school supplies that help with revision—highlighters, colored pencils, big pieces of paper, index cards, and sticky notes.

A revision-friendly classroom means noise, too. Understand that talk—whether it's reading out loud or conferencing over a draft—is an important part of the revision process. Collaboration, with students out of their seats, critiquing, consulting, and creating, is a rich and endless source of new ideas. It's okay. They're working.

Encourage Real Revision

More and more, I find that having students write extremely quick drafts of a piece of writing—skeletons, almost—is a great way to open them to revision. When students are too careful with a first draft, when they've taken the time to check every word in the dictionary as they write, they're often rightfully proud of that work and reluctant to spend any more time on it. Encourage crummy first drafts. Push kids to get ideas down, to write quickly with the understanding that a first draft is the very beginning of a process that is going to go on for a while. Then give them time to walk through that process, and guide them along the way.

Break It Down

Revision is a big word, a big idea, and when we ask students to simply "revise" a piece of writing without spelling out what jobs are involved in that process, it can feel overwhelming to them. Help your students make revision to-do lists. Use the strategies in this book, hand out the Try It pages, bookmark those helpful blog entries to share, and build understanding that the revision process is about doing a bunch of little jobs that add up to one large improvement.

Start with the big stuff—themes, organization, and content—and encourage students to work their way down. Dealing with big ideas before word choice and conventions saves time.

Resist the urge to focus on conventions too soon. I know it's hard. I know that the wrong use of the word *there* drives you crazy. It drives me crazy, too. But try to imagine that you have special glasses that block out errors in conventions when you're reading a student's early draft. Try to pretend it's all invisible and that all you can see are the ideas, the words the student meant to say. Focus on those first, and try to help kids do that as well, because getting caught up in a whole page of spelling errors is the number one way to make sure that more substantial revision never happens.

Reach Out

So many resources are available for teachers who want to have a revision-friendly classroom. For one, consider the other teachers who are working to help their students develop a more meaningful writing process, just as you are. Maybe they're in your school. Maybe you'll need to find them at conferences or online social networks. But do find them—you can share ideas and encourage one another in your beliefs that teaching real revision is worth the effort.

Use real authors, too. Kids who like to read have built-in role models when it comes to writing. Many of these authors talk about process on their blogs, and many are willing to make connections with your students, either through e-mail exchanges or Skype virtual visits. The bigger and more inclusive your

FIGURE 17.1
Future author mentors

classroom writing community is, the more excited your students will be to be part of it.

Who knows? Maybe some of the students you're teaching today will come back as author mentors, signing books and giving advice to your future classes. Maybe it will be that kid in the corner with the sticky notes or those two girls whispering over the story on the computer screen (Figure 17.1). They'll remember that you gave them the time, space, and strategies for real revision and the skills to take their writing to the next level.

Appendix

TRY IT: POLISHING STONES

If revising is like rock tumbling, what do the early and later stages look like? Try this progressive to-do list with your own writing.

Early Tumbling/First Steps

- What did I want this piece of writing to be about? Does it do that job?
- Are there big sections/paragraphs/scenes that don't seem to fit? Cut them.
- Where could I add more detail and description?
- Does the voice of this piece feel real when I read it aloud?

Keep Tumbling/Middle Steps

- Do the characters in my writing feel like real people? How can I make them more interesting?
- Are there factual details that I need to check? Do I need to do a little more research?
- When I think about organization, does this piece make sense? Do the details of the time line work? Could I put the events on a time line or calendar to check?
- Where might I add more detail (again!)?
- Have I included language that appeals to all five senses?

Polishing/Fine Tuning

- Are there extra words that I can cut?
- Are my verbs active and precise?
- Are my nouns specific and concrete?
- Can I get rid of adverbs and replace them with stronger verbs?
- If I read my piece out loud, are there sentences that make me stumble? How can I make those sentences flow more smoothly?
- Finally (when all the other polishing is done), have I proofread my story to make sure I've used correct grammar, spelling, punctuation, and capitalization?

TRY IT: GET PERSPECTIVE

Here are the steps for one author-model you might use as a revision strategy.

- Thinking about big-picture revision ideas (don't worry about minor editing yet!), read through your piece of writing from start to finish, making notes in pen or colored pencil.
- Then go back and make changes on your computer document. If it's a handwritten piece, write a new draft with the changes included.
- Read the draft in one sitting, again, and make changes.
- Then give your manuscript to a friend (he or she can play the role of editor) to make notes as well. Remember that writing questions in the margin is a great way to get yourself or another writer thinking about possible changes!

TRY IT: TITLE TALK

Need a title for your piece of writing? Try to go beyond the obvious by brainstorming in the table below. In each box, write one word that has to do with your story or report. Like Danette Haworth, you'll want to choose the most vivid words that really capture the feeling of what you wrote. Then use a pair of scissors to cut the table so each word is on its own piece of paper. Experiment by moving the pieces around to come up with different combinations. When you finish, you will have a whole new list of title possibilities!

TITLE-TALK BRAINSTORMING TABLE

TRY IT: WHAT IF?

Try author Kathi Appelt's "what-if" strategy to explore some possibilities that might take you in new directions as you revise. Use the space below to come up with at least three "what-if" questions. What if my main character decided to drop out of the spelling bee? What if she gets in trouble on that day, on purpose? Ask those kinds of questions—and then answer them. Ready . . . go!

What if _____?

My answer: If that happened, then

What if _____?

My answer: If that happened, then

What if _____?

My answer: If that happened, then

Real Revision: Authors' Strategies to Share with Student Writers by Kate Messner. © 2011. Stenhouse Publishers.

TRY IT: CREATE A CHARACTER LOVE/HATE CHART

One of the lists in Erin Dionne's notebook was a character love/hate chart that she'd created for her forthcoming novel, *Notes from an Accidental Band Geek.* It helped her explore her main character Elsie's personality by examining the things Elsie loved and hated the most.

What does your character love more than anything? What's at the top of your character's "Hate" list? Use the chart below to brainstorm.

Character's Name_____

Loves	Hates

TRY IT: MAPPING THE SETTING

Get a big, blank piece of paper and some colored pencils and create a map that shows where your piece of writing takes place. Is it a neighborhood? Think about the streets and houses, yards and shortcuts. Is it a fantasy world? You'll need to decide where the lakes, rivers, and mountains are. Once you have the basic world of your piece of writing down on the map, you can start to sketch in little drawings and notes about where important events take place.

Use this strategy for works of nonfiction, too. For research papers about historical events, make a map of the area where the event takes place, and pencil in notes about where the action happened. And understand that maps aren't limited to geographic locations; you can also "map" the human digestive system, a cell, the water cycle, or the layers of the atmosphere as a way to clarify your ideas for informational writing.

TRY IT: SUMMARIZE

What's the most important statement you can make about your piece of writing? Summarize the meaning in one sentence. Once you've found this theme, you will have what Tanya Lee Stone describes as the "mantra" for that piece of writing—the one sentence to which everything else on the page must return. The mantra can help guide your revision process. Here are some examples to inspire you:

Type of Writing	Possible Mantra
Persuasive letter about rain forest preservation	The world's rain forests are an important resource that must be preserved.
Poem about losing a pet	The feeling of missing follows you everywhere.
Personal narrative about winning a swim meet	Determination and lots of practice paid off in one exciting minute.
Short story about two friends who grow apart	People change as they grow, and sometimes old friends don't seem to fit any more.
Research paper about honey bees	Honey bees are an essential insect in nature.

Mantra Statement for My Work-in-Progress: _____
_____
_____
_____
_____
_____
_____

TRY IT: PICTURING YOUR CHARACTERS

Find a picture—photograph, painting, drawing, sketch, or video—of the person about whom you're writing. That should be a simple library/Internet job if you're writing about a real person, but what if your characters are fictional? You can try using a photograph of someone you know or searching for a photo of a real person who might resemble your character. If your character is a girl with blond hair, for example, use whatever search tool your teacher recommends to search for images of "girl with blond hair" and see if one of those pictures looks like the image of the character in your head. Once you "find" your character, search for more details. Is that a birthmark on her chin? Does her hair always stick up on one side? Why is she tipping her head? And what is she looking at in the distance?

Take some time to study the image of your character and write down details. Later, look for good places to weave these details into your writing; you don't want to "dump" all the description in one spot!

TRY IT: DETAILING THE SETTING

Adding more setting details to a piece of writing can save your characters from "floating" and make your readers feel more deeply connected to a story. But sometimes adding those details means returning to research. Here's a quick research worksheet you can use to find more place-based details. Note: Imaginary places need details, too! If your world is a fantasy world or made-up planet, try basing it on a real country or planet. I know authors who base their fairy-tale castles on real castles in France or Germany and authors who have based their dystopian worlds on real-life locations that have experienced catastrophic events, such as Chernobyl.

My setting: _____

Research and take notes to provide details in the following categories:

Geography (mountains, rivers, deserts, oceans, etc.)

Weather (during the time of year when your piece of writing takes place)

Trees, flowers, and other plants that grow there

Insects that might be present (to "bug" your main character!)

Common animals

Birds

Popular foods of that place

Clothing

Other place-related notes for setting details

TRY IT: INCLUDING SENSORY DETAILS

Great descriptive writing appeals to more than just one or two senses. You can train yourself to include sensory details by practicing paying attention to your surroundings and by focusing on one sense at a time. Choose a setting—something as simple as your classroom or the sidewalk outside is just fine—and spend one minute writing only details about what you see. When you finish, turn your eyes "off" and turn your ears "on," and focus only on what you hear. Spend a minute or two writing details that you notice relating to each of the four senses. (Use that fifth sense of taste only if there's actually food present!)

What do you see?	What do you hear?	What do you feel?	What do you smell?	What do you taste?

Real Revision: Authors' Strategies to Share with Student Writers by Kate Messner. © 2011. Stenhouse Publishers.

TRY IT: DRAMATIZE A STORY SCENE

Acting out a scene in your story can be a great way to find more vivid details to include from your character's point of view. Find a scene in your story that might work, and enlist the help of a friend if needed. With a notebook nearby, act out your character's movements. Is he or she falling? Sneaking into a room? What do you notice about how your body moves when you act out the sequence? How does it feel? Jot down those details in your notebook, and then you'll be ready to go back and add them to the scene when you revise.

TRY IT: PUT YOURSELF IN YOUR CHARACTER'S SHOES

When it's not possible to act out a scene from your story, you might be able to find a "substitute activity" like Cynthia Lord's rolling-suitcase walk. Read through your piece of writing. What scene includes an experience you've never had and can't create easily or safely? You may still be able to gather details for that scene with an experience that puts you in your character's shoes.

If your character is being chased, for example, try running as fast as you can, imagining someone behind you. What happens to your body? Your heart rate? What if your character has injured his or her arm by falling into a pit? (I hope this has never happened to you!) Try binding one arm to your side with a scarf and climbing with just your legs and other arm to get a sense of how difficult fast-paced movement might be with those restrictions.

Brainstorm a list of situations in your story with possible substitute activities that might help you to add details!

Situation _____
Possible substitute activity

_____

_____

Situation_____
Possible substitute activity

_____

_____

Situation_____
Possible substitute activity

_____

_____

TRY IT: POINT OF VIEW

How might different people in different moods view your classroom? Try the following writing exercise to find out.

First, write as yourself. Look around the classroom and see what details you notice.

_____
_____
_____

Now try writing as your teacher. What might stand out to you? What might you notice that the student missed? What would be more important to you?

_____
_____
_____

Now imagine you are a time traveler, visiting from the year 1800. What would you notice first? And how would you describe this place?

_____
_____
_____

TRY IT: BE PRECISE

Jeannine Atkins tries to use concrete nouns—specific, precise words—and verbs that really suggest action. Need some practice being precise with your language? Try to replace the underlined general, vague words in the sentences below with more specific, vivid language.

Old: The <u>dog</u> <u>jumped</u> into my lap.

New: _____

_____

_____

_____

Old: My mom made me <u>clean up</u> the <u>junk</u> on my bedroom floor.

New: _____

_____

_____

_____

Old: When I <u>walked</u> into the house, I could smell <u>food</u> cooking.

New: _____

_____

_____

_____

TRY IT: USE VIVID WORDS

Once you've finished making all the big-picture revisions to a piece of writing, print out a copy and do a new read-through with a highlighter in your hand. Whenever you find language that's plain—words and phrases that could be more lively or beautiful—highlight it in the text. Then use a pen or pencil to write in possible word choices that are more vivid, and make those revisions in your next draft.

If you're working on a computer, you can use the highlighter feature in Microsoft Word to mark those words and phrases that could be stronger. Then use the comments feature to make notes about words you might choose as replacements.

TRY IT: CREATE A CHARACTER BIOGRAPHY

Try out the biography sheet that Wendy Mass uses for her novels. Answer as many questions as you can about the main person in your piece of writing.

Character Biography

Character's name_____

Boy or Girl_____   Age_____

Physical description _____

Hair style & color_____   Eyes _____

Other defining physical traits_____

Personality (3 traits) _____

Clothing style_____

Mother (describe in 3 words)_____

Father (describe in 3 words) _____

Siblings (if any) (describe in 3 words) _____

Name of best friend_____

Name of antagonist/enemy/object of conflict_____

Favorite activities_____

Favorite things he/she owns _____

Favorite foods _____

Favorite music_____

Favorite TV show _____

Favorite book _____

Handles problems by_____

Greatest love _____

Bad habits/weaknesses _____

What does your character want more than anything? _____

_____
_____
_____
_____
_____

Real Revision: Authors' Strategies to Share with Student Writers by Kate Messner. © 2011. Stenhouse Publishers.

TRY IT: COLLECT CHARACTER NAMES

Start your own collection of character names. They don't have to come from unwanted e-mail addresses like G. Neri's; names are everywhere. Jot down names of kids in your class that you like. Who has a last name that would make a good first name? The phone book has many names to choose from. Try skimming through the pages, and keep a list of your favorites.

First Names for Girls	First Names for Boys	Last Names

TRY IT: INTERVIEW YOUR CHARACTERS

Go beyond the original biography sheet you filled out for your character and interview him or her. You can do this in writing if you want, or you can even set up a microphone and video camera to record both "sides" of the interview. Here's a list of questions to get you started.

What does your bedroom look like?

What's under your bed?

Who has disappointed you?

What is your secret dream?

What do you want/need right now?

What are some of your favorite songs and why?

If you got really good news, who would you call first?

What do you like most about yourself?

What would your parents say is your greatest flaw?

What would your friends say is your greatest flaw?

What do you believe in?

TRY IT: CREATE HYBRID CHARACTERS

Some of Eric Luper's characters are a hybrid, or mix, of people he knows. Blending qualities of actual people you know is a great strategy for coming up with characters who have realistic traits and personalities. To begin, list three people you know in the column on the left. Then fill in the information about those three people (only positive, kind observations, please!). When you've finished, you can use the list to blend the traits and qualities and create a new hybrid character.

Person's name/ initials	Physical description (hair color, eye color, etc.)	Something the person loves/is good at	Something the person doesn't like	Unusual quirk or detail about this person	Other notes

TRY IT: DRAW YOUR CHARACTER

Write a quick paragraph about your main character's appearance. Now take a few minutes and draw that character, including as much detail as you can. It's okay if you're not an artist! But try to notice the little things about this character—decide which way his or her hair is parted and whether or not it sticks up around the ears. After you've had a chance to finish your drawing, go back and revise your character paragraph to add more details.

TRY IT: MATCH NAMES TO PERSONALITY TRAITS

Brainstorm a list of names that seem to fit certain personality types. What would be a good name for a boy who always loses things? A girl who wants to join the school football team? What about a really tough kid? A particularly nosy neighbor? Brainstorm names for characters (no fair using names of real people you know!), and then compare notes with your classmates to see if they agree.

WHAT NAME WOULD YOU GIVE A . . . ?	IDEAS FOR NAMES
Girl who wants to play football	
Boy who loses things	
Tough kid	
Nosy neighbor	
Mean teacher	
Funny teacher	
Clumsy girl	
Glamorous movie star	
Evil criminal	

TRY IT: REVISE THE DIALOGUE

Dialogue, when a character speaks in his or her own words, reveals a lot about who that character is. Revising dialogue can be a great way to improve character development and consistency throughout the story.

Think about how your character would really talk. What slang might he or she use? Does the character tend to speak in long sentences or short ones? Find all of your main character's dialogue (words in quotes) and copy and paste just that dialogue into a separate document. If you're writing on paper, you can simply highlight it with a marker or colored pencil. Now read just your character's dialogue out loud. Does it sound consistent? Does it sound like the same person talking? If there are lines that don't work well, try out different versions to make the dialogue sound more natural.

TRY IT: GET INSIDE YOUR CHARACTER'S HEAD

What can you do to feel more like your character? How can you get into that person's head? If you're home and you have the right clothing (like the shawl Kathryn Erskine used to feel more like her character), then give it a try and see if it helps you get into that mind-set. Even if you can't dress as your character, you can always journal and talk as your character. Try writing in your character's voice in response to the following prompt. When you're done, try reading what you've written aloud, using your character's voice and expression.

The thing that really bugs me the most is _____

_____

_____

_____

_____

_____

_____

_____

_____

_____

_____

_____

_____

_____

_____

_____

_____

_____

_____

_____

_____

TRY IT: SWITCH YOUR POINT OF VIEW

Take a scene or page from your manuscript and rewrite it in one or more different points of view. Is it written in third person? Try telling it in first person. Is it written in first person? Try switching to third, or use first person but let a different character be the narrator. Read your new versions aloud along with your original. Which one works best?

TRY IT: PUT YOUR SENTENCES ON TRIAL

When it's time to cut words, phrases, and sentences (maybe even whole paragraphs and pages) from your piece of writing, you need to be tough. Olugbemisola Rhuday-Perkovich's question about whether a particular passage is worth fighting for can bring the importance into greater focus. What would happen if you deleted the sentence or paragraph? Would the piece of writing still make sense? Would it be as vivid, quirky, or entertaining? What role does the passage play in your piece?

Imagine that you're standing before a judge who has put your sentences on trial. Your job is to defend them, to go through your story line by line and explain why each sentence must stay. You might find that you can advocate for some sentences but not others. Keep the best and send the others off to be deleted.

TRY IT: GET A LISTENER INVOLVED

Sit down with a partner and explain—without reading your piece of writing—what happens. You might notice that you can't easily summarize the story or the thesis or the message, a sure sign that the point isn't clear in your own mind. Time for some revision. If you are able to recount the story, then ask your listener if he or she has questions or lost interest along the way. Answering the questions and discussing your ideas can help you target the repairs.

 Real Revision: Authors' Strategies to Share with Student Writers by Kate Messner. © 2011. Stenhouse Publishers.

TRY IT: CUT YOUR WRITING TENTATIVELY

Worried about eliminating your hard work in a piece of writing? Try author Julie Berry's method of tentative cutting to take away the sting. If you're writing on a computer, use the strike-through feature (one of the choices under Format-Font-Effects in Microsoft Word) to see what your writing would be like without that phrase or sentence. Then, if you like the change, you can delete the text for good. If you're writing on paper, a light pencil line through the text in question is another great way to "try on" revisions before you actually start cutting.

TRY IT: ASK A "CRITICAL" FRIEND

Questions that "critical" friends raise about our writing can be powerful revision tools. Trade papers with a partner, and grab a pen or colored pencil. Read your partner's manuscript and, in the margins, jot down questions that occur to you as you read. The questions can be simple ("Why would he do this?" or "What was she thinking when this happened?") or more complex ("If she's riding her bike to her friend's house for the party, how could she possibly carry that huge birthday present?"). Afterward, trade papers back and talk about the issues you each raised. Let the reader ask the questions while the author listens, thinks, and then answers. When it's your turn to listen and answer questions, be sure to have a notebook handy so you can remember ideas brought up during the discussion.

TRY IT: PUT ON REVISION HATS

You can take Karen Day's advice literally and dig four or five different hats out of your closet if you'd like—but you can also use this strategy without putting anything special on your head. Make a list of "hats" you think you should probably wear to revise the particular piece of writing you're working on. Some examples of different kinds of writing and the editing hats you might want to wear as you revise them appear on the next two pages. The list includes specific things to look for on each revision pass for that genre.

FOR POETRY	FOR FICTION	FOR A RESEARCH PAPER
Noun-patrol hat: Are all the nouns in this poem specific and concrete?	*Character hat:* Do all the characters feel real, and do they act in ways that are consistent with their personalities?	*Fact-checking hat:* What details do you need to confirm to make sure they're accurate?
Verb-patrol hat: Are all the verbs in this poem active and descriptive?	*Setting-details hat:* Are there places where you could describe the setting in better detail?	*Plagiarism patrol hat:* Have you included phrases that are not in your own words? Be sure to attribute if you need to use a quote; otherwise, rewrite.
5-senses hat: Does the language in this poem appeal to all of the senses?	*Pacing-police hat:* Have you included scenes/ sentences that aren't essential? Would the story work better without them?	*Elaboration hat:* Are there ideas in this paper that haven't been fully explained? Mark them so you can add more detail and elaboration later on.
Extra-word hat: Get rid of every single word that's not doing an important job in the poem!	*Timekeeper's hat:* Do all of the events in the story follow a logical time line that makes sense from one page to the next? Can you put the events on a calendar?	*Organization hat:* Do the ideas that are grouped together make sense together? Is the report easy to follow, and does one idea lead naturally to the next?

FOR PERSUASIVE WRITING	FOR TEST WRITING
Thesis hat: Is the point of your writing clear from the beginning, and does the piece end by restating the same point?	*Question hat:* Have you answered all parts of the question? Underline the parts if it helps!
Prove-it hat: Are there many details and examples given to support each of the ideas put forth? Which ideas need more support?	*Examples hat:* Have you given specific examples from the text to support your ideas as needed? Can you add more?
Consistency hat: Does everything in this paper support the main argument? Are there any facts/details that seem to contradict it?	*Clarity hat:* Is your writing easy to understand? Can someone who's grading it quickly see that you've done the job you were asked to do?
Voice hat: Read out loud when you wear this hat. Does it sound like there's a real person behind the writing? How can you make it more conversational?	*Word-choice hat:* Where could you improve a word choice to make it more specific, more lively, or more vivid?

Resources

Albee, Sarah. 2010. *Poop Happened! A History of the World from the Bottom Up*. New York: Walker.

Angleberger, Tom. 2010. *The Strange Case of Origami Yoda*. New York: Amulet.

———. 2011. *Horton Halfpott*. New York: Amulet.

Appelt, Kathi. 2008. *The Underneath*. New York: Simon & Schuster.

———. 2010. *Keeper*. New York: Simon & Schuster.

Atkins, Jeannine. 2010. *Borrowed Names: Poems About Laura Ingalls Wilder, Madam C. J. Walker, Marie Curie, and Their Daughters*. New York: Henry Holt.

Baskin, Nora Raleigh. 2008. *All We Know of Love*. Somerville, MA: Candlewick.

———. 2009. *Anything but Typical*. New York: Simon & Schuster.

Berry, Julie. 2009. *The Amaranth Enchantment*. New York: Bloomsbury.

Bird, Elizabeth. 2009. "SBBT: Meet Rebecca Stead." Interview with Rebecca Stead. *Curriculum Connections*, May 22. http://blog.schoollibraryjournal.com/afuse8production/2009/05/22/sbbt-meet-rebecca-stead/.

Burns, Loree Griffin. 2007. *Tracking Trash Flotsam, Jetsam, and the Science of Ocean Motion*. Boston: Houghton Mifflin Harcourt.

———. 2010. *The Hive Detectives: Chronicle of a Honey Bee Catastrophe*. Boston: Houghton Mifflin Harcourt.

Collins, Billy. 2002. "Litany." *Nine Horses: Poems*. New York: Random House.

Davis, Katie. 2008. *The Curse of Addy McMahon*. New York: Greenwillow.

Day, Karen. 2007. *Tall Tales*. New York: Wendy Lamb Books.

———. 2011. *A Million Miles from Boston*. New York: Wendy Lamb Books.

Dionne, Erin. 2009. *Models Don't Eat Chocolate Cookies*. New York: Dial.

———. 2010. *The Total Tragedy of a Girl Named Hamlet*. New York: Dial.

———. 2011. *Notes from an Accidental Band Geek*. New York: Dial.

Erskine, Kathryn. 2010. *Mockingbird*. New York: Philomel.

Fagan, Deva. 2009. *Fortune's Folly*. New York: Henry Holt.

———. 2010. *The Magical Misadventures of Prunella Bogthistle*. New York: Henry Holt.

Feldman, Jody. 2008. *The Gollywhopper Games*. New York: Greenwillow.

———. 2010. *The Seventh Level*. New York: Greenwillow.

Fishbone, Greg R. 2007. *The Penguins of Doom*. Austin, TX: Blooming Tree.

Gephart, Donna. 2010. *How to Survive Middle School*. New York: Delacorte.

Goodman, Susan E. 2004. *The Truth About Poop*. New York: Viking.

Halse Anderson, Laurie. 2000. *Fever: 1793*. New York: Simon & Schuster.

———. 2008. *Chains*. New York: Simon & Schuster.

Haworth, Danette. 2008. *Violet Raines Almost Got Struck by Lightning*. New York: Walker.

———. 2010. *The Summer of Moonlight Secrets*. New York: Walker.

———. 2011. *Me and Jack*. New York: Walker.

Holm, Jennifer L., and Matthew Holm. 2005. *Babymouse: Queen of the World!* New York: Random House.

Holmes, Sara Lewis. 2009. *Operation Yes*. New York: Scholastic.

Kent, Rose. 2007. *Kimchi & Calamari*. New York: HarperCollins.

———. 2010. *Rocky Road*. New York: Alfred A. Knopf.

Key, Watt. 2006. *Alabama Moon*. New York: Farrar, Straus, & Giroux.

———. 2010. *Dirt Road Home*. New York: Farrar, Straus, & Giroux.

Larson, Kirby. 2006. *Hattie Big Sky*. New York: Delacorte.

Leitich Smith, Greg. 2003. *Ninjas, Piranhas, and Galileo*. Boston: Little, Brown.

Lord, Cynthia. 2006. *Rules*. New York: Scholastic.

———. 2010. *Touch Blue*. New York: Scholastic.

Luper, Eric. 2009. *Bug Boy*. New York: Farrar, Straus, & Giroux.

———. 2011. *Jeremy Bender Vs. the Cupcake Cadets*. New York: HarperCollins.

Marino, Nan. 2009. *Neil Armstrong Is My Uncle & Other Lies Muscle Man McGinty Told Me*. New York: Roaring Brook.

Mass, Wendy. 2009. *11 Birthdays*. New York: Scholastic.

Messner, Kate. 2009. *The Brilliant Fall of Gianna Z*. New York: Walker.

———. 2010. "Sometimes on a Mountain in April." http://kmessner.livejournal.com/145183.html.

———. 2010. *Sugar and Ice*. New York: Walker.

———. 2011. *Marty McGuire*. New York: Scholastic.

———. 2012. *Marty McGuire Digs Worms*. New York: Scholastic.

———. 2012. *Eye of the Storm*. New York: Walker.

———. 2012. *The Star Spangled Setup*. New York: Scholastic.

Mitchell, Saundra. 2009. *Shadowed Summer*. New York: Delacorte.

Murphy, Jim. 1995. *The Great Fire*. New York: Scholastic.

———. 2003. *An American Plague: The True and Terrifying Story of the Yellow Fever Epidemic of 1793*. New York: Clarion.

———. 2010. *The Crossing: How George Washington Saved the American Revolution*. New York: Scholastic.

Neri, G. 2007. *Chess Rumble*. New York: Lee & Low Books.

———. 2011. *Ghetto Cowboy*. Somerville, MA: Candlewick.

Pattison, Darcy. 2010. "Shrunken Manuscript." http://www.darcypattison.com/revision/shrunken-manuscript/.

Perkins, Mitali. 2010. *Bamboo People*. Watertown, MA: Charlesbridge.

Rhuday-Perkovich, Olugbemisola. 2010. *8th Grade Superzero*. New York: Arthur A. Levine.

Schroeder, Lisa. 2010. *It's Raining Cupcakes*. New York: Aladdin.

Selfors, Suzanne. 2010. *Smells Like Dog*. New York: Little, Brown.

Sensel, Joni. 2009. *The Farwalker's Quest*. New York: Bloomsbury.

Stead, Rebecca. 2009. *When You Reach Me*. New York: Wendy Lamb Books.

Stone, Tanya Lee. 2009. *Almost Astronauts: 13 Women Who Dared to Dream*. Somerville, MA: Candlewick.

———. 2010. *The Good, the Bad, and the Barbie: A Doll's History and Her Impact on Us*. New York: Viking.

Urban, Linda. 2007. *A Crooked Kind of Perfect*. Orlando, FL: Harcourt.

———. 2011. *Hound Dog True*. Orlando, FL: Houghton Mifflin Harcourt.

Wiles, Deborah. 2001. *Love, Ruby Lavender*. San Diego: Harcourt.

———. 2005. *Each Little Bird That Sings*. Orlando, FL: Houghton Mifflin Harcourt.

———. 2010. *Countdown*. New York: Scholastic.

Yolen, Jane. 2010. *Elsie's Bird*. New York: Philomel.

Credits

CREDITS

Page 88: *The Crossing* by Jim Murphy, © 2010. Used by permission of Scholastic Press.

Page 90: *Elsie's Bird* by Jane Yolen and David Small. Cover illustration by David Small. Used by permission of Penguin Group (USA) Inc. All rights reserved.

Page 104: *Tracking Trash* and *The Hive Detectives* by Loree Griffin Burns, © 2007, 2010. Used by permission of Houghton Mifflin Harcourt.

Page 106: *Operation Yes* by Sara Lewis Holmes, © 2009. Used by permission of Arthur A. Levine Books, an imprint of Scholastic, Inc.

Page 108: *Touch Blue* by Cynthia Lord, © 2010. Used by permission of Scholastic Press.

Page 120: *The Candymakers* by Wendy Mass, © 2010. Used by permission of Little, Brown Books for Young Readers, an imprint of Little, Brown & Co.

Page 122: *Yummy: The Last Days of a Southside Shorty*. Text copyright © 2010 by G. Neri. Permission arranged with Lee & Low Books Inc. New York.

Page 124: *It's Raining Cupcakes* by Lisa Schroeder, © 2010. Used by permission of Aladdin Books, an imprint of Simon and Schuster, Inc.

Page 126: *Jeremy Bender vs. the Cupcake Cadets* by Eric Luper, © 2011. Used by permission of Balzer + Bray, an imprint of HarperCollins.

Page 128: *The Strange Case of Origami Yoda* by Tom Angleberger, © 2010. Used by permission of Amulet, an imprint of Abrams Books.

Page 130: "Jacket Cover," © 2010 by Delacorte Press, an imprint of Random House Children's Books, a division of Random House, Inc., from *How to Survive Middle School* by Donna Gephart. Used by permission of Delacorte Press, an imprint of Random House Children's Books, a division of Random House, Inc.

Page 132: *Dirt Road Home* by Watt Key, © 2010. Used with the permission of Farrar Straus Giroux Books for Young Readers, an imprint of Macmillan Children's Publishing Group.

Page 144: *Mockingbird* by Kathryn Erskine, © 2010. Used by permission of Penguin Group (USA) Inc. All rights reserved.

Page 146: *Smells Like Dog* by Suzanne Selfors, © 2010. Used by permission of Little, Brown Books for Young Readers, an imprint of Little, Brown & Co.

Page 146: Suzanne Selfors photo by Kate DeVeaux.

Index